Rosemary Sadlier

Rosemary Sadlier has served since 1993 as the volunteer president of the Ontario Black History Society (OBHS), the first and only provincial heritage organization in Canada focused on African-Canadian history. Under Sadlier's leadership, the OBHS obtained the formal proclamation of February as Black History Month at the Ontario level and initiated the national declaration in Canada, effective December 1995. The OBHS has also initiated the formal celebration of August 1 as Emancipation Day, obtained at the provincial level, and pending nationally.

Sadlier has received many awards, including the William Peyton Hubbard Race Relations Award, a Woman for PACE Award, the Black Links Award, the Planet Africa Marcus Garvey Award, a Harry Jerome Award, the Order of Ontario, and she is a Kentucky colonel! Her previous works, including *The Kids Book of Black Canadian History*, have made her a frequent guest on national television and radio. She is a doctoral candidate of the Ontario Institute for Studies in Education. She lives in Toronto.

In the same collection

HARRIET TUBMAN

FREEDOM SEEKER, FREEDOM LEADER

ROSEMARY SADLIER

DUNDURN
TORONTO

Editor: Jennifer McKnight
Design: Jesse Hooper
Printer: Marquis

Library and Archives Canada Cataloguing in Publication

Sadlier, Rosemary
    Harriet Tubman : freedom seeker, freedom leader / Rosemary Sadlier.

Includes bibliographical references and index.
Issued also in electronic formats.
ISBN 978-1-4597-0150-2

    1. Tubman, Harriet, 1820?-1913. 2. Women slaves--United States--Biography. 3. African American women abolitionists--Biography. 4. Underground Railroad. 5. Underground Railroad--Canada. I. Title.

E444.T82S22 2012   973.7'115092   C2011-903794-7

1   2   3   4   5   16   15   14   13   12

We acknowledge the support of the **Canada Council for the Arts** and the **Ontario Arts Council** for our publishing program. We also acknowledge the financial support of the **Government of Canada** through the **Canada Book Fund** and **Livres Canada Books**, and the **Government of Ontario** through the **Ontario Book Publishing Tax Credit** and the **Ontario Media Development Corporation**.

Printed and bound in Canada.
www.dundurn.com

Dundurn	Gazelle Book Services Limited	Dundurn
3 Church Street, Suite 500	White Cross Mills	2250 Military Road
Toronto, Ontario, Canada	High Town, Lancaster, England	Tonawanda, NY
M5E 1M2	LA1 4XS	U.S.A. 14150

Contents

Preface

I have written this book about Harriet Tubman, her achievements and contributions, because I feel she was an international figure who had an immeasurable impact on our concepts of freedom and justice. Tubman's heroism, spirituality, and selflessness allowed her to become one of the most famous black women in the nineteenth century. Facing overwhelming odds, she managed to fend for herself and guide as many as three hundred "passengers" in the possible nineteen rescues she successfully executed. That she lived in Canada for eight years and that she has Canadian descendants is less commonly known.

My cousin, the late Helen Smith, was instrumental in bringing Harriet Tubman's story to the people of St. Catharines. My colleague, Rochelle Bush, the current historical director also of Salem Chapel, British Methodist Episcopal Church in St. Catharines, has built upon that foundation. It is my hope that this book will bring both the American and Canadian story of Harriet Tubman to a wider audience and provide further insight about this remarkable woman.

I was drawn to this project because I have been touched by the accomplishments of this heroic woman who had no social, educational, or financial advantages because of her birth, race, and gender at that particular time in history. Clearly, if Harriet Tubman could make a difference given all that she had to deal with, we can too.

I wish to acknowledge some of the persons, past and present, who so kindly provided ideas, documents, pictures, oral histories, and referrals which have helped me in the research and writing of this book, particularly the following in both the United States and Canada:

Nancy Assman, historian, Cayuga County, Auburn, New York

Gail Benjafield, St. Catharines Public Library, St. Catharines, Ontario

John Bertniak, Archives, Brock University, St. Catharines, Ontario

Charles Blockson, former curator, Afro-American Collection, Temple University, Philadelphia, Pennsylvania

Dorchester Public Library, Cambridge, Maryland

Pat Fraser, St. Catharines, Ontario

Malcolm Goodelle, archivist, Cayuga County Historian, Auburn, New York

Dr. Daniel G. Hill, Toronto, Ontario

Calvin Kimbrough, Niagara University,
Buffalo, New York

Paul Litt, Ontario Heritage Foundation,
Toronto, Ontario

Ed Patton, Western New York Heritage Centre,
Buffalo, New York

Arden Phair, St. Catharines Museum, St.
Catharines, Ontario

Michael Power, Welland, Ontario

Paul Redding, Kenicious College, Niagara
Falls, New York

Helen Smith, Salem Chapel, BME Church, St.
Catharines, Ontario

Susan Suk, St. Catharines, Ontario

Owen Thomas, Brantford, Ontario

Judy Tye, Toronto, Ontario

Glen Walker, Fort Erie, Ontario

Sheila Wilson, St. Catharines Public Library,
St. Catharines, Ontario

Many descendants of Harriet Tubman shared their time and their stories with me. I would like to thank everyone who unveiled the story of the descendants of Harriet Tubman, in particular:

Betty Browne, Dundas, Ontario

Geraldine Copes, Rochester, New York

Pauline Copes Johnson, Rochester, New York

Laberta Greenlea, Rochester, New York

Joyce Jones, Syracuse, New York

Hazel Martin, Buffalo, New York

Mariline Wilkins, Philadelphia, Pennsylvania

… and their children, grandchildren, and great-grandchildren

(These were their positions/locations at the time of my first contact with them)

Through my mother's family, I am a descendant of those who made their way to Canada through their contact with the Underground Railroad. Because of this I am particularly interested in the courage of these freedom seekers and am fascinated by the ways in which they came to be free. Unfortunately, I am deeply aware of how little information is known or made available about the systems they used. Despite the importance of this heritage being passed down through the generations to contemporary black and wider community members, particularly through oral tradition, many personal experiences of freedom seekers remain hidden forever. Due to the historic nature of many of the quotations in this book, they may contain archaic and unconventional spellings. The publisher has chosen to lowercase "black."

Harriet Tubman was committed to helping her family and this prompted her to carry out several crossings to rescue her relatives. I wondered if perhaps within the fabric of the stories of the Tubman family there would be details that would extend our knowledge of Harriet and the secret routes she used? Or if perhaps her legacy had lived on through the presence of her descendants? Because the descendants might hold the answer to some of the missing pieces, I began a study of Tubman's family legacy, as well as her own historical legacy. I met with many descendants from both the United States and Canada and I have included a section on Harriet's North American genealogy, reflecting her family in both the United States and Canada.

I feel that information about her family is important to our understanding of Tubman, the Underground Railroad, and the settlement of people of African descent. It is important for those who have made the run for freedom and never arrived, for those buried in forgotten or hidden cemeteries without our knowledge, and for those of us, like Harriet, who realize that one person can make a difference.

Introduction

This book will provide some new interpretations and information on the most notable African-American/African-Canadian conductor on the legendary Underground Railroad: Harriet Tubman. Based upon interviews with Tubman descendants, archival materials, and extant literature, this book will acquaint the reader with the experience and contribution of just one of the many notable, identified leaders on the Underground Railroad, placing her in a local, regional, international, and global context.

The Underground Railroad was the first freedom movement of the Americas and is credited with infusing Canada with a number of black people. How did it work? Where did people come into Canada? How were they treated upon their arrival? How is it that we spoke of these things in certain places and why was this missing from the education that I was receiving at school?

The nature of slavery did not lend itself for many to keep detailed records. For slave owners, the date and place of the birth of the offspring of enslaved women was not always recorded and was left to memory. Many now feel that ancestral memory has power; that "indigenous knowledge" has value not always accepted or recognized. However, the selling of slaves had an impact on plantation memory. No one may have remained in your circle who could verify your date of birth, or even your parentage. No one may have realized the need to do so. When an enslaved African was sold, and once that memory was gone, it was as if a library had been lost. The stories about your birth, issues on your plantation, would be lost unless there had been an opportunity for this information to be passed down through African oral tradition or recorded by slave owners.

To this end, there are several dates for Harriet Tubman's birth in the literature. A descendant fervently believed Tubman to have been born in 1820, "if not earlier." Harriet Tubman herself indicated that she was "about seventy-five years old" in 1898 as she was trying to ensure that she receive her back pay for her military service and status as a widow. Was she being modest about her age, or is it that she did not know her exact age and took her best guess? Another famous black abolitionist, Frederick Douglass, took February 14th to be his birth date as he had never been provided with documentation to indicate otherwise.

There were essentially two types of support for the Underground Railroad (UGRR) escapes: the formal and somewhat documented and those activities that happened on the spur of the moment and that were almost acts of kindness or veiled acts of resistance. Even after the UGRR had ended, the fear and real possibility for legal action kept many stories of assistance and involvement secret, and many of the stories literally went to the grave with the involved persons. In modern times the Underground Railroad is often romanticized to the point where it might almost seem to have been a pleasant, albeit lengthy stroll from a place of hard work and restriction to a place of easy opportunity and acceptance. The truth is that the Underground Railroad was a significantly danger-fraught means of escaping from the real threat of severe punishment or death towards the possibility of freedom in various communities in the northern United States, or further on into Canada. In Canada, Ontario was the largest recipient of those "fugitive slaves," those freedom seekers. Who would lead such a perilous journey? Why risk one's life for others? How could she have managed to evade capture? Who was this heroine of legend? How could an "uneducated," "unsophisticated" enslaved African become the person of historic and contemporary notoriety and fame? How can the legacy of one black woman be so compelling that her story resonates across international boundaries? This book will attempt to provide some new insights into the saga of slavery, the mechanisms of the Underground Railroad, what happened to freedom seekers upon their arrival to places usually called "North," and the nature of the character of the person who would become known as a famous freedom seeker, a freedom leader, the Moses of her people, Harriet Tubman.

The economies of many countries, including the United States and especially in the agricultural south, were built upon the labour of captured Africans. Slavery, as experienced by the survivors of the "Middle Passage" between Africa and the New World and their descendants, was all encompassing. They had no rights whatsoever under the law. Enslaved blacks had to work constantly under the watchful eye of overseers who whipped slow workers. They could not legally marry and raise a family, they could not attend school or learn to read and write, they could not live where they wished, follow their interests, or move about in society as they pleased.

Unlike the slavery imposed by other societies at other times, this servitude was lifelong and perpetual. If children came about through acts of breeding, acts of love, or acts of violence they were automatically enslaved. And, because Africans had distinctive dark complexions in a society where free people usually were white, their skin colour immediately identified them as being a slave no matter where they were. Their African names, religions, histories, languages, customs, and families were taken from them by the time they were auctioned off. They were required to use the name given to them by their owner and work a hard job for which they received no salary and little recognition. Over time certain slaves started to be freed, perhaps because of guilty consciences, because a slave's value had decreased due to old age or poor health, changing attitudes about slave owning, or because the dark complexion and distinctive features of the captured Africans started to approximate the colour and appearance of their owners due to forced intimate relations. The northern states, with their large Quaker settlements and anti-slavery proponents, tended to free slaves earlier than other areas. This pressured neighbouring states and Canada to struggle with the debate about abolishing slavery or continuing it.

In 1793 the cotton gin was invented and was widely used. It permitted the plantation owner, through the work of his slaves, to more quickly and efficiently remove the tiny seeds from cotton. This resulted in much more profit for the owners. Because the free labour of the slaves was so valuable to their owners and to the agricultural economy of the south, those who relied the most on exploiting them tended to be the white southerners who had large land tracts that they could not profitably manage to cultivate without slavery — free labour.

In the same year the first fugitive slave law in the U.S. came into force and it allowed slave owners or their agents — bounty hunters or slave catchers — to bring any black person before a magistrate and accuse them of being a runaway. With the vague descriptions of freedom-seeking slaves that existed, any black persons who were so accused and not able to provide immediate proof of their free status were forced to be returned to their "master."

The first enslaved African, Olivier Le Jeune, was a young boy who was brought into Canada in 1628. Slaves were held in Canada only by the wealthy to do household work, livery work, barbering, and laundry, but this was mostly due to the fact that large-scale plantations did not exist in Canada, so fewer slaves were needed there. However, no matter how many slaves there may have been, slavery was still a dehumanizing process that reduced Africans who had contributed to the process of civilization to mere beasts of burden. Slavery had negative repercussions for that period of history, which have continued through to the present day as evidenced in negative treatment or perspectives about people of African descent and the erroneous idea that only Europeans contributed to civilization. Slavery was abolished in Canada on August 1, 1834, which is known as Emancipation Day.

Black people did not want to be slaves, and fought against it as well as they could. Some resisted passively, by intentionally working extra slowly, pretending not to understand commands, or discreetly contaminating or poisoning food. Many slave revolts are documented, but trying to run away was extremely difficult. Slaves would be tracked down like animals by groups of men with guns and dogs, and they were further disadvantaged by not necessarily knowing where they could go, or who could help them. If caught alive, slaves would be returned to their master where some sort of punishment — a foot or an ear hacked off, an eye removed, or a severe whipping — would be administered to leave the freedom seeker able to work, but unable to attempt another escape. It also signalled to other would-be runaways the punishment they could expect for trying to escape. When it was easy to obtain slaves, the runaway might have been hung, but as the importation of captured Africans slowed down in the nineteenth century, torture, branding, disfigurement, and maiming were preferred to destroying "property." Stolen labour was so valued by owners of large plantations that in Virginia in the 1850s officials started to consider enslaving "poor whites."

Human dignity and free choice were unimportant, especially when wealth could be amassed by dehumanizing and exploiting others. Slaves lived in separate shacks away from the big house or mansion where the owner lived. Their homes had dirt floors and possibly one thin blanket for a bed. Meals were plain, served from a pot, and eaten with hands. For example, slaves ate cornmeal porridge, fish, or "pot liquor," the liquid left after vegetables are cooked. The stolen "discards" from slaughtered pigs and cows would supplement their rations. The discards consisted of heads, intestines, organs, feet, and tails, as would squirrels or other small animals that industrious, hungry black people would catch. If they became ill they had to nurse themselves back to health as no doctor would be summoned for them. Knowledge of herbal remedies from the African tradition or learned from Native People was indeed valuable.

Mothers might be able to have their children with them in the evenings, but even children were taken into the master's house to assist or were hired out to work for others at the whim of their owner. Parents and children, brothers and sisters, husbands and wives could at any time be permanently separated from each other by being sold, and they often were. In fact, some owners felt that people of African descent had no feelings and did not care if their children were taken from them. Pro-slavery forces felt that enslaved Africans accepted and actually *preferred* to live their lives in bondage. There was little comfort for slaves except each other.

Work might slow down on Sundays as Christian owners and overseers would not work on their Sabbath day. Religion was given to the slaves only to reinforce their inferior position and justify their abuse. If a slave died, he or she could only be buried at night because the master's needs for the labour of his slaves always came first, well above the emotional trauma felt by the slave community over losing a loved one. The images of freedom and movement in many of the hymns did help to provide images of a life that might be had possibly in the North or after death. Those hymns became codes for people who were willing to follow the call for freedom.

The Underground Railroad was born of the desperation and resolve of black people to be free, and the commitment and resources of free blacks and whites to end slavery. The Underground Railroad was the name of a means of escaping slavery through using various trails, safe houses, and vehicles. It was a system of people helping people to be free, but being connected to the Underground Railroad was dangerous. The Underground Railroad "carried" its human cargo from the late 1700s until slavery was abolished in the United States beginning in 1863. It was the busiest from 1850 on because of the passing of the second *Fugitive Slave Act*, which put all blacks, whether free-born, manumitted (granted their freedom in the Will of their owner), or runaway, at risk of recapture no matter where they were in the United States. By this time, many of these black peoples had been free for several generations and had acquired considerable property. If they resisted being re-enslaved they were beaten or killed. Some black families were even kidnapped in the middle of the night.

A "ride" on the Underground Railroad would not be comfortable. Your conductor would lead you north on foot by night through swamps, paths, river shores, and forests. If you were lucky, you would have part of your passage on a real train or a boat paid for or provided by abolitionists — but you might have to wear a disguise since you could end up sitting beside someone who could identify you. You might travel from one station to another in a secret compartment of a wagon or on a makeshift boat. Your food would consist of whatever you had been able to carry and whatever you could find during the six to nine weeks your trip could take. Your sleeping quarters might be a hollow tree, a culvert under a bridge, a cemetery, a root cellar, a barn, a cave, or the open terrain. Until you reached your final destination, you would be in constant fear of being recaptured.

Many died along the way or soon after reaching the land of freedom because of starvation, chronic fatigue, or exposure. Before 1850, you only needed to travel to places like Philadelphia in the northern United States, but after 1850 your trip would have to be longer, likely all the way to Canada, therefore the risk of recapture would be greater. You would "buy" your ticket with your commitment to be free at any cost, including leaving your family behind, and you would "claim" your luggage of liberty with your first steps into Canada.

* * *

There are two concepts that describe the large-scale capture and sale of millions of African people: the slave trade and *Maafa*. Maafa comes from the Swahili word for "disaster" and refers to the African Holocaust. For five hundred years Africans were captured, enslaved, and brought to areas controlled by Europeans and Arabs. This ongoing enslavement of Africans had an impact on African settlements and systems, African ways of knowing, African religions, African languages, and the whole gamut of further potential developments within Africa and within the African diaspora. Maafa had an impact on how Africans were perceived, where Africans were felt to be in relation to whites, and on the ways in which Africans were categorized according to the depths of their melanin, their skin colours, rather than on other factors. The slave trade is about how profit was made; Maafa is about the impact on African peoples.

Africans had made their way to North America independently prior to enslavement. Their remains have been found in the Olmec areas of Middle America and on some of the islands in the Caribbean dating back as early as 800 A.D. Africans travelled into the areas now known as Canada and the United States with the coureurs de bois, fur traders, in the 1400s. Black people helped to found Chicago and built Ontario's first parliament building in the 1700s. Their presence in North America "before Columbus" is documented, but their routine inclusion in North American history does not usually begin until the transatlantic slave trade.

Africans were often hired as interpreters to work with Europeans doing business in Africa. It was not uncommon for an African to be able to speak French, Dutch, or Portuguese in addition to their native tongue. Canada's first named African was Mathieu Da Costa, who arrived on Canada's east coast by the early 1600s. A free black man, Da Costa was a translator and contract negotiator for Samuel de Champlain, a French trader and explorer who was on a voyage of discovery with Pierre Du Gua de Monts. Through Da Costa's linguistic skills and possible previous visits to Canada, he was able to interact between the First Nations (the Mi'kmaq and Montagnais) and the Europeans, creating a relationship. Mathieu Da Costa has been commemorated in Canada by the Federal Government since 1996 for his efforts to establish a link between and among the various early arrivals to Canada.

The first known enslaved African to arrive in Canada was an eight-year-old boy captured from Madagascar and brought to Quebec by David Kirke, a British Commander, by 1628. Sold to a French clerk, Olivier Le Baillif, the child remained enslaved. In 1632, the French regained control of the area, and Le Baillif left, giving his enslaved child to Guilliame Couillard. Being sent to a religious school, the child was later baptized and given a formal name, Olivier Le Jeune.

While slavery was not officially legalized in New France/ Quebec until 1709, the practice had been going on for years prior and was an almost international standard. If one was an African, a negro, then one was presumed to be a slave. The Underground Railroad was a clandestine, loosely organized anti-slavery system. Called the first freedom movement of the Americas, it supported the bravery of enslaved people to escape their bondage through the immediate departure from the plantation and supported them as they required hiding places, food, and clothing along the way. Some aspects of the UGRR have been well documented, and those figures, consequently, are well known. However, at the other end of the spectrum, there was much ad hoc assistance provided by any number of persons to fleeing fugitive slaves, so the real numbers will never be known. More than random acts of kindness, the providers of this help, whether it be a bit of food, correct directions, looking the other way, or actively escorting enslaved Africans, were all knowingly directly contravening the law. Assuming terms from the rail system, station masters were in charge of safe houses, conductors led people through parts of their journey, passengers were the escaping people, and stockholders were those who contributed or handled fundraising for the purchase of necessary supplies for runaways.

1

Harriet Tubman's Beginnings

Harriet Tubman is one of the most well-known figures connected to slavery and the Underground Railroad. Her story is the continuation of one that had its beginnings much earlier, on the continent of Africa, the ancestral home of all black people.

Harriet Ross Tubman was one of the most famous conductors on the Underground Railroad. She was not content with being free after her escape from the Brodess plantation when so many others were still in bondage. She risked her life to make numerous trips into southern slave-holding states, to rescue family members and others. Her courage, strength, and dedication to fighting slavery led her to join the Union side during the American Civil War. Throughout the war, Tubman acted as a nurse, scout, and military strategist.

Harriet Ross Tubman was one of the youngest of the eleven children born to Benjamin (Ben) and Araminta (Rittia, "Rit") Green Ross in Dorchester County of Maryland's Eastern Shore around 1820. Harriet Ross (later Tubman) was born a slave since both of her parents were slaves; Rit was owned by Edward Brodess (also spelled Brodas or Broades) and Ben was owned by Dr. Thompson. The marriage of her parents' enslavers brought Ben and Rit together on the same plantation. Harriet's great grandparents belonged to the Ashanti tribe and were captured from Central Ghana in 1725. This made Harriet the fourth generation of her family to be enslaved in the United States.

When Harriet was very young, she was free to run about the plantation while her family went to work in the fields. Young enslaved children were cared for by slaves who were too old to do the more strenuous work. Each year the slaves were issued their clothes and Harriet received her rough cotton smock, but nothing else, just like the other slave children. No shoes were given to slaves, and Rit, like the other enslaved adults, received plain outfits or the used clothes of the master's family and his staff. To keep warm on chilly evenings, Harriet would snuggle up to her mother as they, along with the rest of the family, tried to sleep on the dirt floor of the tiny place reserved for them as a home. At least Harriet had the benefit of warm, nurturing parents and the security of being in the same place as her family, as many children were sold away never to know what had happened to their parents or brothers and sisters. Something as simple as a birthday was not given any recognition, so slaves knew little of their African heritage, little of their family heritage, and little of their personal heritage.

From *The Refugee* by Benjamin Drew, Harriet Tubman said of her life:

> I grew up like a neglected weed, ignorant of
> liberty, having no experience of it. Then I was

not happy or contented: every time I saw a white man I was afraid of being carried away. I had two sisters carried away in a chain-gang — one of them left two children. We were always uneasy.

Now that I have been free, I know what a dreadful condition slavery is. I have seen hundreds of escaping slaves, but I never saw one who was willing to go back and be a slave. I have no opportunity to see my friends in my native land, if we could be as free there as we are here. I think slavery is the next thing to hell. If a person would send another person into bondage he would it appears to me, be bad enough to send him to hell if he could.

By the time Harriet was about five, it was decided that she should be hired out to other people. Brodess would charge for Harriet's services and keep the money that Harriet earned. As was the custom for slaves, she took another name when she was hired out, calling herself Araminta or "Minty." For this substitute owner, Harriet was to clean all day and rock the baby all night. Because she was a slave, not a "person," her need for sleep was overlooked. Her mistress wanted to make sure she got her money's worth out of her slave, even when the slave was scarcely older than the child she was expected to care for. She dusted and swept to the best of her ability, but because some dust remained in the room she was whipped about her face, neck, and back. This process was repeated four times until her mistress realized that Harriet needed to be shown how to do it correctly. Until the day she died, she bore the marks of these and subsequent beatings. Harriet detested indoor work; she detested slavery. In order to rock the baby, Harriet had to sit on the floor since the child was almost as big as she was. If the mistress was awakened by the cries of the child, Harriet was beaten. When Harriet was returned to her mother because she was ill, her mistress said that she had not been worth a penny.

On another task, Harriet was to learn to weave, but the fibres in the air bothered her — she did not do well. Then the master, James Cook, had Harriet tend his muskrat traps in the nearby Greenbriar swamp. Harriet preferred to be outdoors, away from the constant glare of the mistress, but she soon became sick and feverish due to the insects and dampness of the swamp. Her master demanded that she continue to work, but when Harriet was unable to she was returned to Rit to regain her strength. Slaves were not considered people or citizens of the land they toiled, so Rit's knowledge of helpful herbs and her almost constant care got Harriet through her bout of measles and pneumonia — no doctors were summoned for "property." Harriet later said that her owner, Brodess, was not unnecessarily cruel, but those to whom she was hired out to were "tyrannical and brutal."

Harriet was deprived of many of the things that her owners took for granted. When she was hired out to a family near Cambridge to do housework, young Harriet was tempted to try one of the sugar cubes she saw in the sugar bowl. She noiselessly removed one cube and popped it into her mouth, but she was convinced her mistress had seen her stealing. Fearing punishment, she ran away, hiding in the pig sty. She hid for five days, eating the same food that the pigs ate. This was not too difficult to do since in certain respects it was better than what she was normally given to eat. Finally, she came out of hiding and was whipped for running away.

Harriet was described as a willful and moody child — perhaps she was trying to express her independence. She was adamant about having outdoor work, so Brodess relented. At least he would be able to get some more money from her outdoor work instead of having other owners sending her back all the time because she was a poor house worker. As such, nine-year-old Harriet was hired out to do field work. This was an area that Harriet did well in. She enjoyed the outdoors, the feeling of almost being free since she was not being closely monitored. Luckily for Harriet, because she proved valuable in harvesting, tilling, and planting, she was not used for breeding purposes. Harriet's outdoor work also had the side benefit of strengthening her petite body and increasing her endurance, which would later serve her well on her treks north.

Being outdoors with other travelled slaves brought Harriet into contact with stories of escaping slavery, and she learned that freedom could be had by following the northerly flow of the Choptank River out of Maryland or by following the "drinking gourd," which was the North Star. In this same way, she learned that the nature of enslavement in the deep south (Alabama, Georgia, Louisiana, Mississippi, and South Carolina) was decidedly different, the work more taxing and ongoing, the conditions and punishments often even harsher.

> When the sun comes back, and the first Quail
>   calls,
> Follow the drinking gourd, For the old man is
>   a-waiting for to carry you to freedom
> If you follow the drinking gourd.

Chorus:
Follow the drinking gourd,
Follow the drinking gourd,
For the old man is a-waiting for to carry you to
    freedom
If you follow the drinking gourd.

The riverbank will make a very good road,
The dead trees show you the way.
Left foot, peg foot traveling on,
Following the drinking gourd.

The river ends between two hills,
Follow the drinking gourd,
There's another river on the other side,
Follow the drinking gourd.

When the great big river meets the little river,
Follow the drinking gourd.
For the old man is a-waiting for to carry you to
    freedom
If you follow the drinking gourd.

While Harriet's owner may have been, in comparison to other slave owners, "fair," he did treat his slaves harshly mainly because he developed financial problems. To raise money, he abruptly sold two of Harriet's older sisters, Linah and Sophy. This act not only separated the sisters from Ben, Rit, and their other brothers and sisters, but also left two of Linah and Sophy's children behind. This was the norm for slaves, but it made Harriet decide early on that she would try to take control of her life, that she would be free.

This woodcut shows a heartbreaking scene in which a mother in bondage is wrenched from her baby to be taken to the auction block and sold away. Harriet's older sister Linah was taken away in this fashion, never to be heard from again.

2

Wedded Bliss

The practice of hiring out slaves to other owners also impacted couples, since legal unions for enslaved people were not allowed. Some "marriages" between slaves amounted to one or two annual visits a year because the partners might be owned by masters living 100 miles or more apart or by masters who had to shift their slaves to those areas where there was work for them to do. Maryland had a law that stated that there were no rights for blacks that a white person had to respect, which included marriage vows. The very ability to choose your own partner and consider yourself married, to "jump over the broom," was a fortunate position — to live with your partner was less likely unless you were both free or both enslaved on the same plantation.

Harriet Tubman was fortunate to have both of her parents in her life as well as her siblings since each of her parents' owners had married. Harriet Tubman was hired out to work on other plantations because the economic factors in the north had changed. Where once the crops grown in the Maryland area were highly labour intensive, such as harvesting tobacco, by the nineteenth century the focus shifted to grain and timber for the growing ship-building industry in Baltimore for both local consumption and export. Neither of these products required the ongoing labour of a full complement of slaves.

This economic reality, coupled with the religious imperative to free enslaved people, facilitated a rise in the free black population — formerly enslaved Africans who were manumitted, or given ownership of themselves. They were free to hire themselves out to those planters who had need of temporary assistance. It also made the sale of one's property, one's slaves, to the demanding needs of the south in the sugar and cotton plantations, very lucrative. Following the War of 1812, European products increased competition, further pressuring the American economy and making the lure of selling one's slaves seem even more appealing.

"Slavery is terrible for men; but it is far more terrible for women. Superadded to the burden common to all, *they* have wrongs, and sufferings, and mortifications peculiarly their own."

— Harriet Jacobs,
Incidents in the Life of a Slave Girl

The experience of being a slave was different for men and women. Initially, most enslaved Africans were male in order for them to carry out the extremely hard work that required great strength. Over time, African women were included to provide both company for the male slaves and for the potential to have an ongoing supply of slaves. Until 1808, the reliance on American-born enslaved people was small, since up until that time it was possible to obtain robust young slaves directly from a slave auction. Female slaves were sold at a reduced rate, so they were favoured for their ability to do agricultural work in order to make up for the male labour assigned to building and carpentry, blacksmithing, and clearing fields.

Both male and female slaves might be given the same work on a very large plantation, which created another layer of loss for the enslaved person. Traditionally in Africa women would hoe a field. A woman's work in the field would be for the benefit of her children and her community. What did it mean for a man to hoe a field? How would he have felt in doing this? What did it mean for a woman to assume some of the more demanding work, such as when Tubman would later work with her male relatives cutting and preparing timber? How were the traditional roles of men and women changed during enslavement?

In addition to being subject to the needs of their enslavers in relation to the type of work they had to perform, enslaved African women were subject to having their bodies made available to their owners. It did not matter if the female was only a young girl or a married woman, her body was owned by the enslaver. Enslaved women were forced into premature sexual knowledge due to the advances and rapes made against them by their owners and then subject to abuse by the owner's wife who would blame the enslaved woman for the advances made on the slave. Marriage was no protection. So common was the rape of married women that many enslaved African men hoped to find a mate on another plantation lest they have to witness the humiliation, harm, or violence perpetuated against their partners should they be fancied by the owner or the object of persecution of the slave owner's wife.

Enslaved women might be enticed by the promise of freedom for themselves or their children. They also could have threats made against them or their family members if they refused to be willing participants in an emotionless physical relationship. Should the enslaved woman wish to marry someone she did love, it may not be granted by the owner. If an offer came in from a free black to buy her freedom so that she could leave, it might also be refused. In Missouri, one enslaved African teenaged woman's story centred on her final decision to kill her owner, Robert Newsome. Celia (also known as Margaret Garner) had been sexually abused to the point where she hit her owner in the head, then kept a fire going all night to consume his body. At the time, it was decided that she had "no reason" for killing her master. She was pregnant with her third child by him.

Pregnancy might provide the enslaved woman with additional food or potentially lighter work, but did not free her from being punished should she displease the overseer. Special pits were dug so that the full belly of the pregnant slave would fit into the hole while she lay down with her back exposed so that she could be whipped without harming her growing child. Where motherhood was a positive community event in African societies, during enslavement it was a bit different. The mother might be removed from her child early on, or at some point see her child sold off, perhaps never to be seen again, or might see her own daughter raped. Enslaved women bore a child almost every two years, with lengthy nursing preventing more frequent conception. The mother may have seen several of her children die in infancy due often to poor nutrition, infection, or disease.

From first contact, where African women were captured, examined, and sold, any number of men might rape the potential slave. It was felt to be their right, part of their entitlement in assessing the potential productivity of their purchase. Once sold, forced encounters and/or alliances grew between owners and enslaved women, women who hoped to gain certain advantages for themselves, their families, and, more importantly, for their children. Pregnancy, whether due to rape, marriage, or consensual union had the same result for the children in most of the United States. Laws were passed that made the child of an enslaved mother a slave no matter if the father was a free black or a white person. Some children born of these circumstances would be sent north to live as free people or to Europe to be highly educated as other children of the same white father. However, it was more common for the owner's children to become house servants in his own home, or willed to a close family member.

Due to the way that enslaved African women were forcibly taken, the children the women bore could not just be their child, but could also be their sibling, their grandchild, or their cousin. It was about violence against the body, control, and incest. As long as the child was at least one sixteenth black, the child was considered to be black, and therefore subject to enslavement.

Since early African arrivals were initially considered indentured servants, they were allowed to serve their terms of indenture and then petition to be free just like the English, Scottish, and Germans were allowed. Should there be any children, they could be free as well. The laws quickly changed so that indenture did not end and enslavement was formally established.

Following a notable case in Virginia, a woman born of a free white father and an African mother claimed her freedom through her status as the daughter of a wealthy white man, and did not serve her term. By 1662, the concept of *Partus sequitur ventrum*, a legal doctrine, was applied so that any child born of an enslaved woman would be a slave. This set the tone for this type of relationship and made it possible for white men to avoid having any responsibility for the children they sired with African women. Not only was this a financial savings for the owners, it reduced the potential for scandal and relegated their promiscuity to the plantation, not "refined" society.

Because enslaved African women were subject to the confinement and control of their enslavers and their sexuality was fantasized and "available," black women were seen as being more willing to be sexual in relation to white women, who were seen to be "pure." Many wealthy slave owners alienated their white wives in their pursuit of and involvement with enslaved African women. The children born of these unions were sometimes treated with special care by the male owner who might not be able to bear selling them. However, should the wife remain in the picture, her treatment of the "other woman," the enslaved African and her "mulatto" child, was not so charitable.

Having the lighter skinned slaves in the house to do the lighter work and the darker skinned slaves in the fields was due to the fact that the lighter ones were the owner's children. It also had the effect of further colourizing class. In trying to find ways to further care for one's own children, white plantation owners supported the establishment of the "black" universities where their offspring could be educated.

Having children bound the enslaved woman to the place where her children were. It made it more difficult for her to contemplate escape since her children might not be easy to spirit away from the home of the owner, the care of the older slave women, or the glare of the mistress of the plantation. Similarly, having the enslaved male marry was seen as means of tying him to the plantation, although it made it difficult for him to attempt to protect his wife from violent threats to her — both physically and sexually — as he could not betray his master. What did this do to his sense of self as a protector when he could not intervene in the treatment of his wife?

Part of slave resistance included enslaved people's finding ways to worship, celebrate, or socialize with each other. Using remote locations, invited through secret communications, they could have services or "parties" that would serve as an opportunity to either practice traditional spirituality or to have some fun, dance, and sing. These brief times away allowed for some courting and friendships to be extended. It provided fleeting moments of freedom. It informed those who would be able to choose a partner.

Harriet chose free black man John Tubman to be her partner. She may have become acquainted with him as he travelled or through one of the secret meetings in the woods. After their union, it would appear that no children were born to them. It is possible that a head injury may well have affected Harriet Tubman's ability to adequately produce the hormones necessary for reproduction. Without having children to worry about leaving behind, and with her small frame built up through hard work as well as her knowledge of how to determine directions and survive outdoors, Harriet was as well positioned to run away as any man.

3

Unearthing the Truth

During fall evenings, field slaves would work in a group to clean up the wheat and husk the corn. One fall evening in 1835, Harriet saw a slave named Jim, from the neighbouring Barret plantation, make a run for his freedom. Curious, Harriet as well as his overseer, McCracken, chased him. Jim went into the Bucktown general store and was cornered by McCracken, who demanded that Harriet tie Jim up. While Harriet refused, Jim bounded out the door and Harriet blocked the doorway. McCracken responded to this act of defiance by picking up a two pound weight and throwing it, perhaps intending to get Jim, but it got Harriet, hitting her in the forehead and nearly killing her.

For months, Rit did everything she could to help Harriet as she fell in and out of consciousness. Brodess wanted to sell her, but no one wanted the slave who had recurring bouts of sleeping attacks, sometimes as many as four per day. After

Harriet Tubman U.S. postage stamp, thirteen cents. First issued in 1978.

Photo courtesy Milton S. Sernett, Harriet Tubman: Myth, Memory, and History (Durham, North Carolina: Duke University Press), 2007.

she "recovered," Harriet went back to work in the fields for her temporary master John Stewart, and continued to be hired out to Dr. Thompson. Harriet commanded fifty to sixty dollars a week, while a male slave could expect one hundred to one hundred and fifty dollars a week for the same type of work.

Because Edward Brodess was not yet old enough or experienced enough to assume the responsibilities of plantation administration, John Stewart, a builder, had been brought in to take over for a time. Dr. Thompson's father owned Benjamin Ross, Harriet's father, and was Edward's guardian. Harriet drove oxen, carted, and plowed when working at home, and she sometimes worked with her father, who also worked for Stewart. Stewart liked to brag about Harriet's strength because he claimed that she could lift a barrel filled with produce, or pull a plow just like an ox could.

Benjamin Ross, though still a slave, was now a timber inspector and supervised the cutting and hauling of timber for the Baltimore shipyards. If she was working with her father, Harriet would cut wood, split rails, and haul logs, producing half a cord of wood a day. Brodess permitted Harriet to keep a small portion of her earnings, and she used the money left over after giving Brodess his share to buy a pair of oxen, worth forty dollars, to help her in her work. It was unusual for an enslaved woman to be doing a man's strenuous job and even more unusual for a slave to buy and own anything. The Bucktown community would have been aware of this unique slave.

Harriet's narcolepsy, or sleeping seizures, as a result of her near fatal head injury, prevented her sale to southern plantation owners who might not have been tolerant of her sleep attacks. It also kept her from being paired off to breed while an adolescent, as did her plain appearance on her five foot tall frame. Harriet is reported to have looked like she could not understand anything at all at times, and this was very helpful to her since she could assume this "dull" stance around her master or overseers, while taking in everything that was going on around her. Sometimes she even pretended to be having a sleep attack to learn more about her master's plans. In fact, many slaves came to know the plans of their owners, as they would listen and watch them intently while seeming not to be aware at all. "One mind for the white man to see, another mind I know is me."

Harriet was a very spiritual person. Both Ben and Rit possessed a strong faith in God which Harriet shared. They, along with other plantation slaves, worshipped at open-air services at what is now the site of the Bazel Methodist Episcopal Church in Bucktown. By the time of her head injury, Harriet began having visions which guided her or which gave her encouragement. She prayed about everything and took the meaning of her visions to be the response of God to her prayers. She combined an African spirituality with her interpretation of Christianity.

Recuperating also provided her with time to think through the impact of slavery on her life and how she could change her status. Harriet replaced her work name of Araminta with her birth name of Harriet while she was a teenager — though some researchers feel that Harriet was known as Araminta until she was married. Her surname changed when she married John Tubman. John's surname was from his great grandparents' bondage experience with the wealthy Tubman family of Dorchester County. John's parents had been manumitted, freed upon the last will and testament of Justice Richard Tubman. Harriet again was unconventional in marrying a free person.

Certainly Harriet did not wait until her 1844 marriage to consider how to become free. Harriet had been interested in her own freedom for a long time. She questioned John about his freedom and how his parents were manumitted. John's mother had been manumitted so he was free through the freedom of his mother. Only children born of slaves were seen as slaves according to the law. John's mother was granted ownership of herself, manumitted, as a reward for a lifetime of loyalty and hard work.

Slaves could also pay for their freedom by buying their own value as labourers, but this was more difficult to do since wages paid to hired workers were incredibly low. Harriet earned only forty dollars a year after giving Brodess his 98 percent share, and it would take her twenty-five years to buy her freedom if her value did not increase, or if her master did not raise her price. White people who owned slaves did so to benefit from the labour that they could provide. Black people who owned slaves were usually successful in raising the funds necessary to buy their still enslaved family members from their owners and consequently become black slave owners in the process.

Harriet decided to have a lawyer look into the will of Athon Pattison (sometimes written as Patterson), since the Pattisons owned Rit and her ancestors before the Pattisons married into the Brodess family and brought their "property" with them. One of Harriet's ancestors on her mother's side was her grandmother, Modesty. Modesty came to the United States on a slave ship from Guinea and was sold to the Pattisons. Athon's will gave Modesty's girl, Rittia, to his granddaughter, Mary Pattison, the wife of Joseph Brodess. For the five dollars she paid her lawyer, Harriet found out that her mother had wrongfully been kept in slavery and that she was also entitled to be free. "I give and bequeath unto my granddaughter, Mary Pattison one Negro girl called 'Rittia' and her increase until she and they arrive to 45 years of age." Instead of being manumitted, Rit was passed down to Mary and Joseph's son Edward. Instead of being free, "Rittia and her increase" were still enslaved. This made Harriet resolve to be free and to see her family live in freedom.

A "free" state was a state north of the Mason-Dixon line — the boundary between Pennsylvania and Maryland, the boundary between the northern Union States and the southern Confederate States. In the free states, slave holding was not allowed by law. The free states came into being in 1777 and included Maine, Vermont, New Hampshire, New York, and Pennsylvania. As a compromise for allowing California entry as a free state, greater strength was given to the enforcement of slave laws to appease the slave states. The passage of the *Fugitive Slave Act* of 1850 meant that these free states were no longer safe for black people, and they could be captured, tried, and found to be runaway slaves, therefore sent back to slavery. As a result, Ontario and, to a lesser extent, Quebec and the Maritimes became magnets for freedom seekers.

4

Freedom Seeking

Harriet heard that her master, Edward Brodess, planned to sell her and two of her brothers "in the chain gang to the far south" as soon as she recovered from one of her lengthy illnesses. Harriet did not want to be separated from her husband and family, and she did not want to be part of an even more difficult work situation in the south. Picking cotton was back-breaking work. With her sleeping spells she would surely fall behind in her harvesting duties and this would result in her being severely punished. Often agricultural workers in the south would have their day's harvest weighed and there was an expected quota for a worker. She would not survive long under those conditions, because she would be unable to remain alert and working for her entire day in the field. Being sold south would be a certain death sentence for Harriet and she knew that. Harriet had been praying for "the dear Lord to change that man's (Edward Brodess) heart and make him a Christian," to make him a more humane and reasonable individual, but she changed her prayer when she learned of his continuing plans to sell her. She then began praying, "Lord, if you ain't never going to change that man's heart, *kill him*, Lord, and take him out of the way, so he won't do no more mischief."

Edward Brodess died on March 7, 1849, after a lengthy illness. He willed his possessions to his wife Elizabeth. Ben had already been manumitted, but Rit remained a slave as she was too old to be sold profitably. Harriet took the death of her master as a powerful answer to her prayer and it reinforced her faith. She then was warned by a slave on another plantation, who had overheard the business plans of her owner, that she and her brothers were very soon to be sold further south since Elizabeth was not interested in farming on her own. This news, combined with her recurring visions of lovely white ladies with welcoming outstretched arms waiting for her in the land of freedom, forced Harriet to act. For Harriet there was only one choice: she should have been free, she desperately wanted to be free, she felt she had God's support. The threat of being torn from her family to uncertain conditions in the south where there would be no tolerance of her sleeping fits, as they might be interpreted as insolence, was added incentive and she convinced herself to seek her freedom.

From the time she had learned that she should have been free, she had hoped to persuade her husband John to escape with her. Unfortunately, he was not interested in leaving and threatened to tell Harriet's master of her plans to leave. This gave him more control over Harriet — he was free, and if there was a problem between them he could always threaten to tell her master. The times they shared together after his refusal were very tense, and he was constantly watching her to see if she would attempt to run. As much as she would have liked to share her dream with him, and her firm intent to leave, she knew that she could not. She had to be on her guard on the plantation and with her partner right up to the moment that she would leave. Initially she had planned to flee with her two brothers and they set out for the north, but their overwhelming fear of recapture and punishment forced the trio to return. Fortunately their brief, nighttime absence had not been seen by the master. Two days later Harriet set out on her own after singing a hymn to alert her niece, Mary Ann, of her intentions to be free through the coded message and the double meaning of the lyrics she sang while giving a nod or a meaningful look to the listener:

> When dat ar ole chariot comes,
>> When that old chariot comes
> I'm gwine to lebe you,
>> I'm going to leave you
> I'm boun' for de promised land,
>> I'm bound for the promised land
> Frien's, I'm gwine to lebe you
>> Friends, I'm going to leave you.
> I'm sorry, frien's, to lebe you
>> Farewell! oh, farewell!
> But I'll meet you in the mornin',
>> Farewell! oh, farewell
> I'll meet you in the mornin',
>> When you reach de promised land;
> On the oder side of Jordan,
>> For I'm boun' for de promised land."

Mary Ann understood that Harriet was running, but as a worker being watched by the mistress in the big house she did not show any sign that she knew Harriet was leaving. As soon as she was able, Mary Ann alerted Harriet's parents and brothers and sisters. John Tubman would have found out later because he lived off the plantation. Even married slaves, like Harriet, had to return to their master's plantation during the night after being hired out all day — marriage meant that "spare" time (i.e. Saturday nights and Sundays, unless the master had other plans for your time) might be shared between husband and wife. When John did suspect Harriet had left, he advised her mistress of Harriet's interest in finding freedom in the north.

Harriet may have carried a homemade quilt admired by a Quaker woman that she had chanced to meet on an errand for Brodess. This woman promised Harriet that if she ever needed help to contact her. Whether or not Harriet had such a quilt is immaterial — there were many Quakers in the area where Harriet found herself and they were as a group, by that time, resisting slavery. Harriet found this woman early in the days after her escape and traded the quilt for a piece of paper with two names on it, probably the names of other Quakers living further north. Harriet had been told to sweep the yard until her contact's husband came home in the evening to avoid arousing the neighbours' suspicions.

Both the Quaker couple and Harriet had put themselves at risk. Since slaves were considered property, running away was viewed as stealing valuable property from the owner. A slave in search of their freedom was committing a felony, stealing his or her desired labour and those who helped were assisting in theft. If caught, a slave could be maimed, disfigured, or killed as an example to others; those who helped could be harassed, isolated, fined or jailed and infrequently, severely beaten or killed. Running away was not the sort of thing that black women usually did to resist slavery. It tended to be a man's form of resistance. Because of the stake that women had in the care of their children, or because they were working so closely supervised in the master's house, the absence of enslaved women would be noticed quickly. To rebel against their enslavement, enslaved women might poison food, injure livestock, pretend to be ill, or even harm the children of the master. They resisted slavery utilizing the tools and opportunities that were possible in their situations.

Running away required knowledge of where to go, physical stamina, and outdoor survival skills that women slaves may not have developed. This made Harriet Tubman seem an unlikely figure to run since she was only 5 feet tall, she seemed to be unintelligent, she had sudden sleeping attacks, and she was a *woman*. But her physical condition, aside from her sleeping seizures, was good; she was a very strong individual. Her experiences working in the fields had equipped her with a knowledge of nature, a knowledge of survival skills, and the idea that she might succeed. Her strong religious convictions made her feel, like Joan of Arc, that she had God's support for her plans.

Many members of the Society of Friends, the Quakers, lived in the Dorchester County area, and though they had held slaves previously, they had decided as a religious order not to hold slaves by 1776; they were among the early opponents of slavery. Later, the Methodists and the Baptists would free their slaves through manumission. The Underground Railroad was fully operational by the time Harriet got on board. When the Quaker husband got home, he drove Harriet, in a covered wagon, to the outskirts of another town. From there Harriet travelled on her own, following the Choptank River west to the Chesapeake, which ran north to Baltimore, then Delaware and finally freedom in Philadelphia!

Harriet Tubman may have heard from other slaves about which direction to travel, and she may have gotten a ride away from Bucktown, but she had to rely on her own courage and initiative to leave the plantation and her own wits and cunning to avoid recapture. She travelled by night and hid by day. She could not read or write so she had to determine which direction she was travelling by the North Star or by the moss growing on the north side of trees. She avoided obvious routes such as well travelled roads and tended to travel through swamps and rivers since running water, as she phrased it, "never tells no tales."

Harriet was very intuitive. She had strong spiritual/religious convictions, and she always felt a divine presence that assisted her in anticipating danger, knowing whom she could approach for food and shelter, and in finding strength to continue despite feeling discouraged, hungry, tired, cold, and wet. She later said:

> ... there are two things I had a right to — liberty or death; If I could not have one, I would have the other; for no man should take me alive; I should fight for my liberty so long as my strength lasted and when the time comes for me to go, the Lord would let them take me.

Harriet would have been able to find many who would help her in the Camden, Maryland, area since it was the centre of Quaker abolitionist activity and there were many free black "conductors" to assist people along the Christiana River into Wilmington, Delaware. The Mason-Dixon Line, which separated the ideologies and geography of "north" and "south," was just a short distance from Wilmington. Once over the "line" it was possible to meet with abolitionists who might provide assistance in reaching Philadelphia. When Harriet had finally crossed over the line, the political boundary that separated slave-holding state from free state, she was awestruck.

> I looked at my hands to see if I was de same person now I was free. Dere was such a glory ober everything, de sun came like gold trou de trees, and ober the fields, and I felt like I was in heaven.

Philadelphia was a booming metropolis in the 1850s and was the centre of progressive social thought and social action. It was the capital of the United States and had the largest population of free blacks in the Union. While Harriet did not purchase or rent her own home, she did live with friends. The centre of the black community of Philadelphia included Pine, South, 6th (now known as Richard Allen), 7th, and Lombard Streets. It was likely within this area that Harriet met William Still, a staunch black abolitionist. By the 1850s Still was the head of the Pennsylvania Anti-Slavery Society who aided "fugitive slaves" and freedom seekers to travel further north. So dedicated was he that he took the time to record as many details as he could about each of the possible sixty persons a month that passed through his hands in Philadelphia. In addition to their names and freedom names, he was interested in their biographies, their escape story, and their potential destination. He realized that his records, which he was forced to keep hidden, might assist in the next phase of freedom seeking: family reunification. His own family had been separated by the bid for freedom taken by his parents, two of his own brothers had to be left behind and were later sold into the deep south, so through his own knowledge of the distress, he proactively kept the practice up. The impact of his activity is startling. First, among the many persons he interviewed, he realized one day that he was speaking to his own long-lost brother Peter Still. Secondly, after years of burying his material to secure and hide it, he subsequently had it published, adding to our knowledge of the many whose stories were captured in his book, *The Underground Railroad.*

The area of Philadelphia that Harriet arrived in was, and still is, home to Mother Bethel African Methodist Episcopal (AME) Church on the oldest plot of land continuously owned by African Americans in the United States. Harriet Tubman is known to have worshipped at Mother Bethel AME. The first church structure was actually a blacksmith's establishment which was pulled by free black people to the corner of 6th and Lombard. This was followed by another structure, and a third building — Harriet's church — before the fourth and final place of worship, which now exists. The tomb of its founder, Reverend Richard Allen, forms part of the museum in the lower level, and his great-great-great-granddaughter, Catherine Dawkins, is among his descendants in the congregation currently.

The 1800s were a time when Christianity was the religion practised by most of the non-Native peoples of North America, although attempts were also made to convert the Natives. Going to church was an activity that just about everyone would do. Even the slaves were encouraged to worship in their own way, often without too much interference from slave owners.

Laws and social practices strongly reflected the importance of Christianity to the people in positions of power. No one worked on Sundays, for example, because it was viewed as a holy day and it was assumed that members of the community would be attending church services, which could last most of the day.

The Church dictated the spiritual and moral conduct of the era. Leaders in the various denominations of Protestant churches were often influential in the broader social, political, and cultural life of the community. Richard Allen was motivated to form a separate, black church because of his treatment in the "integrated" Philadelphia church he attended. Blacks were to remain in the balconies of the church, while whites could sit on the main floor. Enraged by this lack of true Christian spirit and a lack of being treated as an equal child of God, he decided to test this point by sitting on the main floor, but he was dragged from the church for this breach of conduct. By 1794, he formed the African Methodist

Photo courtesy the Cayuga Historical Society.

The AME Zion Church on Parker Street in Auburn, New York. Tubman worshipped there during the last few decades of her life.

Episcopal (AME) Church, which expanded and provided an example for others. In 1830 he led the first African-American convention, which was dedicated to anti-slavery. Later, freedom-seeking Africans arriving in Canada, especially in Ontario, would form AME churches that were familiar to them after their religious experiences during captivity.

For some American communities, blacks were only allowed to congregate for religious purposes, so many black community leaders were people who had received some religious instruction or were people, usually men, who had assumed a role in spiritual guidance. Sometimes a black minister was the only person in an area who could read so that he could read the Bible to others or keep people apprised of developments affecting the black community from his reading of the newspapers. In some parts of Ontario, African-American ministers of the AME convention served as itinerant ministers, having a circuit of several small congregations if a minister was sent from the American body and if the weather permitted regular travel to some smaller outposts. Over time, these smaller AME circuit churches that struggled to have a weekly service were absorbed by the British Methodist Episcopal (BME) Church.

In Canada, there developed a split between those who were comfortable in continuing to use the AME name with its American affiliation, while another group felt it important to be distinct from the Americans and to align themselves more fully with the British under whose protection they had found security. By 1854, a motion was passed at the AME Annual Conference to form a separate church. In September 1856, the British Methodist Episcopal Church of Canada was first formed in Chatham, Ontario, under the guidance of Reverend Willis Nazrey, a former AME bishop. BME churches sprang up across Canada, as well as Bermuda, although BME churches are currently only operating in Ontario. The BME Church of Canada is now the oldest continually black Canadian owned and black Canadian operated organization in Canada.

5

Leading Others to Freedom

Because of the relatively large free black population and the supportive atmosphere that blacks experienced due to the strong anti-slavery community spirit, freedom seekers came to Philadelphia by water and land after reaching Virginia, Delaware, and Maryland. Enslaved blacks knew that freedom was possible in the northern United States because they had listened to dinnertime conversations about events off the plantation while pretending not to be paying attention. They also knew about freedom in the north because the affluence that the labour of so many slaves provided the master also allowed the master to travel around the northern United States and Canada, taking trusted slaves with them. Slave owners had the luxury of time and money, so they could indulge their passions for hunting, fishing, or visits to rustic spas or retreats.

Enslaved people were told many exaggerated stories about life in the north to discourage them from trying to leave. Even when slaves were told by their masters that all abolitionists spoke French and would make them worship idols or would boil them and eat them, or that nothing grows in the north except perhaps black-eyed peas, that blacks were executed, or that rivers and lakes were thousands of miles wide, that the climate was too cold and severe for a descendent of Africa, their own eyes, their own experiences, and their own connections told them something quite different. One freedom seeker, Lewis Clarke, reported after his determined escape that he was advised that he would have his head skinned, that Canadians would eat his children, poke out their eyes, and have the hair of his children made into collars for their coats. Still they came, despite this horrendous propaganda, because they detested slavery and they knew the truth.

Sometimes enslaved Africans travelling with their masters would be secretly advised by the free black people they would encounter that they could also achieve their freedom by crossing the river at a particular point into a "free" state, a state that had abolished slavery, or by following the North Star just a little further to Canada. If these newly educated slaves did not seek their freedom immediately because of concerns for their family still in bondage, they kept this information for future reference and passed it on to others. When these travelled slaves would return to the plantation, they would convey this knowledge to others. Even though slaves were not supposed to congregate in groups larger than five, there were ways of surreptitiously conveying information from one to another, from one plantation to another, sometimes through religious songs, hymns, spirituals, or messages with double meanings. Slave owners tried to scare slaves into remaining in bondage through misinformation to avoid the time and expense of a search party or bounty hunters, but their efforts were futile, as thousands took their chances on seeking their freedom in the north.

Every enslaved African who made it into free territory did not have to encounter Harriet Tubman to get the "directions" — they were shared by many Africans, First Nations, and abolitionists. However, not all were successful at running away and remaining clear of recapture or settlement in a secret maroon enclave. Harriet had proven success at making her way from the Maryland area into Philadelphia. Harriet was self-reliant — readily able to find work, accommodation, and advice while feeling relatively secure in this setting. However, after a time of taking jobs and quitting jobs to ensure that no one would have the opportunity to identify her as a runaway and to experience the meaning of freedom and personal choice, Harriet began to feel lonely. She compared herself to an incarcerated man who returns home after twenty-five years to discover his home, family, and friends are gone and forgotten.

> I had crossed de line (of freedom) of which I had so long been dreaming. I was free; but dere was no one to welcome me to de land of freedom, I was a stranger in a strange land, and my home after all was down in de old cabin quarter, wid de ole folks, and my brudders and sisters. But to dis solemn resolution I came; I was free, and dey should be free also; I would make a home for dem in the North, and de Lord helping me, I would bring dem all dere....

During the early part of 1850, Harriet saved all her money earned from her positions as cook, seamstress, housekeeper, laundress, and scrubwoman in the hotels and private homes of Philadelphia and Cape May, New Jersey. She had initially resolved to free her family, for she did not think that they would leave on their own, but later she began to think of making a return trip, going back into slave-holding areas on her own to free other slaves. She would not be content until all of her people were free.

Harriet tried to stay informed about her relatives in the south. To do this she made contacts with free black and white abolitionists. Because they could read newspapers describing events or pending slave auction, and because they could write coded letters to individuals that Harriet identified, or to other abolitionists in the south, or through word of mouth, Harriet was able to keep tabs on her family. This is how Harriet was able to learn that her niece (some reports refer to her as a sister) was near Baltimore.

Harriet devised a plan to rescue her niece, Mary Ann Bowley. She asked someone to write a letter to Mary Ann's husband, John Bowley, a free man. Harriet advised him that she would conduct Mary Ann to Philadelphia if he could get her to Baltimore. In December 1850, the rescue plan was almost thwarted by the sudden intent of Mary Ann's master to sell her at an auction in Cambridge. Harriet quickly developed an alternative plan that involved hiding Mary Ann in Cambridge even while the bidding was taking place on her and later spiriting her out of the area to freedom in a six-horse wagon. Harriet's first rescue was successful. Mary Ann was later reunited with her husband and children in Chatham, Ontario.

Harriet may have borrowed passports, called "freedoms," from the free black residents of Philadelphia to assist her with

Mary Ann's rescue and other rescues. A freedom was like a passport that free blacks were required to carry at all times that verified their freedom to anyone who demanded to know their status. She may have identified government workers who were willing to look the other way and allow rescues to occur or who would accept bribes for their silence. Harriet extended her connection to William Still, who would have been able to assist her. William Still was the executive director of the General Vigilance Committee.

Clearly, Harriet's desire to see her family free, her knowledge of who could help her and how, and her success in freeing Mary Ann, likely with the assistance of her brothers, prompted her to attempt another rescue. But with the passing of the *Fugitive Slave Act* in 1850, Harriet said, "After that, I wouldn't trust Uncle Sam wid my people no longer, but I brought 'em all clar off to Canada."

This time Harriet targeted her brother John Ross and his sons, Harriet's nephews, who were in Talbot County, north of Dorchester County. John started out with two other slaves, but he had to leave his sons behind because they could not be isolated from their owner. Because John Bowley had authentic free-freedom papers, it was decided that he should return for John Ross's sons. Bowley was able to kidnap the boys in 1851 and send them back to their self-emancipated father with the assistance of Harriet's planning and contacts.

The third rescue that Harriet attempted was to bring her husband, John Tubman, to Philadelphia to join her in the home that she had made for them. Even though Tubman had not been supportive of Harriet's dream of also being free, and even though he told her master that she had run away, Harriet still loved him. She was bitterly disappointed to find that he had taken another wife, Caroline, and was hurt when they laughed at her suggestion that she could conduct them north. Because of John's rejection, she became even more determined to find happiness in helping others. She also had a large family that needed to be freed. She decided that she would not be content until all of her people in bondage were free.

Harriet found ten slaves who were interested in fleeing north and she conducted them on to freedom. So, in the fall of 1851, Harriet began her third rescue. Her experience and advice prompted her to start out from the south on a Friday, or, more commonly, Saturday night. Slaves did not have as stringent a routine on Sundays because their overseers had the day off, so their absence would not be immediately noticed or acted upon. Handbills and newspapers alerting the community that there were runaways could not be printed until Monday at the earliest because Christian printers closed their businesses on Sunday.

Harriet Tubman travelled by night and rested by day to further avoid detection. She was now a seasoned escape artist and motivator for freedom seekers. However dedicated to freedom Harriet may have been, there were times when "passengers" on her train doubted her ability to escort them north in safety, and who could believe this short, plain woman with sudden sleeping attacks could successfully get them to freedom? She often tried to motivate and assuage fears through singing songs familiar to her passengers, but when that was not enough she was known to pull out her lethal sharpened clam shells and threaten, "Live north or die here!" Harriet Tubman later said of a passenger who wanted to return to his plantation after joining Harriet's rescue party, "If he was weak enough to give out, he'd be weak enough to betray us all, and all who had helped us, and do you think I'd let so many die just for one coward man?"

Harriet was the primary conductor on her freedom train, and she took her responsibility seriously.

6

Arriving in Canada

By 1850 the more powerful *Fugitive Slave Act* had been passed in the United States. It stipulated that any black person could be arrested as a suspected runaway slave if a white person accused them anywhere in the United States, and the charged black person could not testify on their own behalf or be represented by a lawyer. In other words, now there was no safe place in the United States for those who had been free because they had been manumitted or self-emancipated. In the eyes of the law, if you were black, you were likely an escaping slave who ought to be captured. If you had achieved some measure of wealth through hard work, your business, home, or assets might seem attractive to someone who would then accuse you of being an escaped slave. It also stated that any person aiding a runaway slave could be fined $1,000 or face six months in jail. To make matters worse, the special commissioners who chaired the hearings were paid on the basis of their verdicts. They received twice the amount of

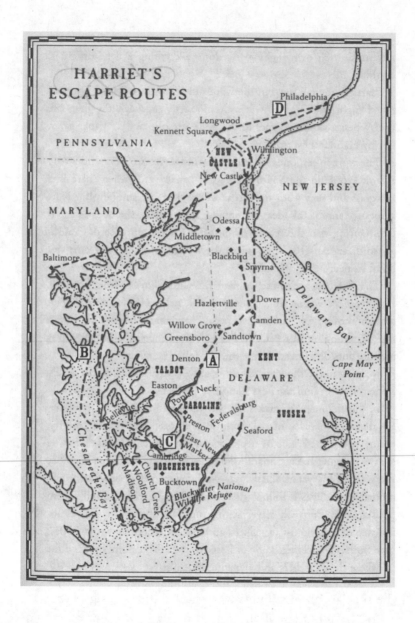

HARRIET'S ESCAPE ROUTES

A

This was probably Harriet's favourite route: from Polar Neck in Caroline County to Denton and then into Delaware; from there up to Wilmington, home of Harriet's friend, the Quaker abolitionist Thomas Garrett, and from there across the Pennsylvania state line to Philadelphia.

B

The daring route of James and Kessiah Bowley and their children, from the courthouse steps in Cambridge and into the Choptank River on a small boat, in which they rowed their way into the Chesapeake and up to Baltimore, where Harriet awaited their arrival in order to whisk them on to Philadelphia. Afterward they made their way across New York State and into Canada.

C

The route from Cambridge to Polar Neck, which Harriet used when facilitating rescues from Bucktown and other Dorchester communities.

D

From Philadelphia, Harriet travelled through the Delaware Canal and down the Chesapeake to Baltimore, where she gathered up Tilly. The two women then went by steamboat even farther south, beyond Cambridge to the southern Dorchester County line, where, after passing through the Hooper Strait, they steamed up the Nanticoke River to Seaford, Delaware, then took a land route north to Wilmington, and, finally, Philadelphia.

money for every black person they sent back to the south and perpetual slavery than for the ones who were freed. It was therefore more profitable for them to return someone to slavery. This made Canada seem to be the only viable refuge for American blacks because the legal and social system which had provided some measure of support for free black people now clearly was being used against them.

Many incidents of racial intolerance and riots also occurred during this period in the northern States as the competition for manual labour or any wage labour became more competitive since immigration from Europe was increasing. Harriet, her passengers, and her family were at terrible risk. Canada presented itself as the closest location in which to find freedom, although other British possessions within the Caribbean and South America were potential sites, but not as easy to travel to. Harriet had travelled on her own two feet; being self-reliant, Harriet would want to take a route that she could walk the whole way if she had to, a route that allowed her many options in arriving at her goal. Canada seemed a good choice, not only because it was close and because it would be possible to walk to this destination, but also because of a series of laws and events within Canada that had given the impression that Canada truly welcomed slaves and would respect their rights to remain free under the law.

The first African to reach Canadian shores was a free black, Mathieu Da Costa, serving in the capacity of translator, and he arrived as early as 1604. The first slave arrived in 1628. So people of African descent had long been part of the fabric of what we now call Canada. While large-scale plantation use of African Canadians was not common, they did provide personal and domestic services for affluent and prominent individuals in all the major cities of the time. The black population grew slowly and steadily following the American War of Independence and the War of 1812, until certain events accelerated this rate.

Black men had been invited to join the ranks of the British forces by Lord Dunmore in 1775 to help to overcome the rebels in the American colony. Sir Henry Clinton invited all blacks, whether fighting men or infirm, women or children, to come to the British side by 1779, and they were promised they would receive the same treatment and rewards as white Loyalists for fighting the rebels. The *Upper Canada Abolition Act of 1793* provided that any slave that came into what we now call the province of Ontario would be free, whether being brought in by a master or brought there by the force of the slave's will to escape bondage. Any child born of a slave mother would be free by the age of twenty-five. William Osgoode, Chief Justice of Lower Canada, declared in 1803 that slavery was inconsistent with British Law. The Cochrane Proclamation aimed at the white and black refugees of the War of 1812 and invited Americans to become British citizens through residence in British Possessions which included Canada, the West Indies, and Bermuda. The *British Imperial Act of 1833* abolished slavery throughout the Empire, including Canada. This act became effective August 1, 1834. And, at the North American Convention of Colored Freemen, held for the first time outside of the United States in Toronto in September 1851, it was decided by black peoples that Canada was the preferred choice for black emigration from the United States because free black people within Canada would be able to assist the fleeing former slave population. Canada seemed to be a safe haven for enslaved black people wanting their freedom and for free blacks desiring a more secure lifestyle because it seemed to be a place where the rights and privileges of the African population would be protected. It was close enough to walk to, the climate was similar to that of the northern United States, there were opportunities to become self-supporting, and Canadians spoke English, the language that most enslaved Africans had become familiar with during enslavement in the United States.

Beginning in the 1830s, free black people and other abolitionists often met at conventions. Initially these gatherings allowed people to share their concerns and to plan ways to end slavery. Interested black people would invite others to their city to have these meetings.

One of the most important of these meetings was the North American Convention of Colored Freemen held in St. Lawrence Hall in Toronto from September 11–13, 1851. It started a trend of discussing black nationalism and emigration of enslaved Africans to Canada. Called by many Ontario black residents such as Henry Bibb, editor of the *Voice of the Fugitive*, and James Theodore Holly, an American-born free black who was devoted to emigration, the convention concluded with the agreement that Canada was a preferred destination for freedom seekers. Other options, such as the West Indies or Africa, were too far from black abolitionist centres in the U.S., and Canada was a more convenient location from which to initiate the escapes of slaves or to assist in the establishing of African-Canadian settlements. Canada, in the eyes of the black community, was considered to be a "beacon of hope" to the enslaved.

When Harriet decided to make her fourth rescue to get her brother James Ross, his wife, children, and nine others, the trip was longer and more dangerous. After stopping at the home of black abolitionist Frederick Douglass in Rochester, Harriet likely made her way to St. Catharines, Ontario, in December 1851 with eleven fugitives.

Frederick Douglass was a self-freed former slave who hailed from Maryland like Harriet Tubman. Unlike Tubman, who suffered a disabling injury as a young woman, Douglass was secretly taught to read by his owner's wife while a young man. In this way he came to learn about other abolitionist stances and about *The Liberator*, the paper of William Lloyd Garrison, a white anti-slavery worker. Ultimately making himself free through the use of a sailor's uniform with "free papers," Douglass married and began to give rousing public speeches, later to write about his experiences as an enslaved African. His autobiography, *Narratives in the Life of Frederick Douglass*, was a bestseller and reprinted several times. He would write a paper, *The North Star*, that would challenge the readership of the Garrison paper and became an advocate for women's rights. Following the Civil War, he was appointed Consul General to Haiti.

However, for Harriet, Douglass also had some valuable contacts in many of the cities that became a part of Harriet Tubman's routes to Canada. From his first steps as a free man, he was acquainted with David Ruggles in New York, initially staying at his safe house. From his women's rights activities he knew the co-founder of the American Anti-Slavery Society, James Mott, his wife Lucretia (Lucretia having relatives in Rochester), and Elizabeth Cady Stanton. Other abolitionists or station masters would include John Hooper and Stephen Meyers in Albany (the Meyer home is being restored as an example of a black abolitionist abode) and Jermaine Loguen in Syracuse.

Courtesy Friends Historical Library of Swarthmore College, Swarthmore, Pennsylvania.

Some of Harriet's helpers. From left to right: unidentified woman (possibly Eliza Wright Osborne's daughter), Martha Coffin Wright, Eliza Wright Osborne (Martha's daughter), and Lucretia Mott.

While some freedom seekers were comfortable in remaining in some of these northern cities, others opted to head all the way across the Canadian border. This would have them enter Canada at Niagara Falls. However, since it was so close to the border at Niagara Falls, a safer option was to go further inland to St. Catharines, Ontario. Harriet Tubman met with Douglass in Rochester and headed to St. Catharines because of a well-known contact, Reverend Hiram Wilson. Wilson had been working with refugees first in Dresden, Ontario, then in the Niagara area for several years.

In addition to the human landscape, there was the physical landscape that presented an excellent opportunity for Harriet Tubman and to anyone wishing to have a fairly direct route to the Niagara area. The canal system of New York State and in southern Ontario provided good secret highways for freedom seekers and the canal systems were fairly well established by the 1850s. Tubman could make her way to Troy, New York, and from there travel east along the route of the Erie Canal. This route would have her touch the tips of the Finger Lakes under the shroud of cover provided by the canal trench and the human connections. If her connections were able to respond to her request for assistance, that would further facilitate her journey. Ultimately crossing at Niagara, a freedom seeker could make their way without as much need for secrecy since crossing into Canada provided freedom under the law. However, should there have been a need to be extra cautious, freedom seekers could have also followed the Welland Canal north from Port Colborne into St. Catharines. With the construction going on for its second stage, the movement of new arrivals would scarcely have been noticed.

* * *

Many blacks had settled the Niagara Peninsula before 1840. As a group they were tolerated and accepted, primarily for the manual labour they provided at a low cost. At times, despite their hard work, thriftiness, and industriousness, they were in need of assistance or were in a position where they needed donated food, especially when they first arrived in Canada. At the time of the Mackenzie Rebellion of 1837, the men, black and non-black, left their families for military duties. So when a group of white women gave the "coloured ladies of St. Catharines" some highly rationed sugar and tea, it was not just enough for them to say thank you, but it became an item for the newspapers! Even though the assistance was sporadic, and not really enough to have kept black people from starving if they were impoverished, there was a certain expected type of behaviour that sympathetic whites wished to see. Blacks were to be overly grateful for every courtesy extended to them, even by people who considered themselves to be abolitionists — the supposed progressive, liberal, activist element of society. Mary Ann Shadd, a black investigative reporter and editor, felt that anti-slavery advocates were more inclined to expect this degrading behaviour than the regular population who might be less supportive of the black community. Said of this ad hoc charity by Shadd, "[The charity of white abolitionists displays] this disgusting, repulsive surveillance, this despotic, dictatorial, snobbish air of superiority of white people over the fugitives."

In June 1852, a group of black military men were parading and, without provocation, were attacked by a group of white young people who also damaged or destroyed homes within the African-Canadian community. The sight of black men in military uniform invoked angry feelings since it was seen by the white youth as demeaning to the uniform. And, because blacks had a role in peacekeeping with the canal workers and in halting the illegal importation of goods from the United States, they were further resented as officers and as African Canadians. The town of St. Catharines voted in 1853 to pay for the damages to the black settlement caused by this riot.

At St. Thomas Church, a black churchgoer, Augustus Halliday, felt that he had to take Communion last so that he would not offend other white churchgoers who would not want to use the Communion cup after him — this even by the 1900s and even though he was a property owner on Wellington Street. His concern was very real and appropriate for the recent historical and social experience of being a person of African descent in St. Catharines. A stained glass window depicting St. Thomas was dedicated on September 10, 1905, in the honour of Mr. Halliday who left money to the church in his will.

In 1867, a young black woman who was employed at the Stephenson House, another of the city's spas, attempted to buy a ticket for the mineral baths, which were supposed to have therapeutic properties, and was refused admission. In an editorial in the *St. Catharines Journal*, some attitudes about African Canadians using public facilities are reflected:

> … the managers would be extremely foolish to allow any such person to bathe with the guests of the house … for there are few who are willing to meet him [the black person] on terms of equality … So long as the coloured man behaves himself in this country he will be respected, but when he presumes to dine at a public house, or to wash in

the same bath as a white man, he is going a little
too far, and public opinion will frown him down.

As long as the growing black population applied themselves to their work and made themselves as unseen as possible, there would be no problem. And with the 1840s arrival of
European immigrants who were also eager to work, the interest in tolerating or supporting people of African descent was
waning. After all, by the time of the 1863 abolition of slavery
in the United States and the 1865 end of the Civil War, many
people may have felt that the blacks could now go *home*, back
where they came from, or, at the very least, someplace else. It
was a time of white encouragement for blacks to resettle in the
Caribbean Islands, Africa, or remote outposts as if their usefulness had been outlived, as if they were not rooted to the soil
they had tilled, as if they were not entitled to live in the country that they had chosen or were born into. Black people were
now discouraged from remaining in Canada, but the choice to
remain was as challenging as the choice to return to the United
States. Freedom in Canada did not also mean full and meaningful employment, full and regularized living arrangements,
equal and appropriate education and training for the young, or
the possibility of living as if they were the same as anyone else.
Though coloured people envisioned their broad entitlement of
the same full freedoms granted to others, their race and history
did not make this a reality.

The *Common Schools Act* of 1850 allowed for the creation of
separate schools for blacks and Catholics. While blacks wanted
to send their children to the best equipped or the nearest schools,
white residents protested the integration of schools, so the act
was used to create separate institutions. Advertisements in the *St.*

Catharines Standard required teachers with a third-class standing qualification teach at the coloured school, while white students would be taught by teachers with no less than second- or first-class standing. Black parents used the power of the vote to defeat an unhelpful school trustee who was felt to be supportive of segregated schools. Protests continued until 1873, at which time the St. Catharines Committee on School Management reported that "mixing coloured and white children in the same classes would prove destructive to the efficiency of the school."

Schools in St. Catharines were later integrated despite the concerns of a few about the effects of social contact between the races. It is important to note that the population of St. Catharines included some families of Native Canadians who lived among the descendants of Africa or Europe. These families were sometimes families of mixed heritage, so the schools that these children attended may have reflected the perceptions of the time regarding racial classification. Clearly, larger settlements of Native peoples existed in other areas of southern Ontario, especially near Brantford.

7

Life in St. Catharines

The central location of St. Catharines, protected in the lee of the Niagara Escarpment, had made it the most populated Native Canadian area in Canada early in history. Its picturesque site was attractive to the first settlers who arrived during the American War of Independence as Loyalists. However, there was a need for water power to help with the running of mills. This led to the initiative by William Hamilton Merritt to follow through on the 1793 proposal of Robert Hamilton to create a canal from the Welland River, near Lake Erie, up to Lake Ontario. On October 24, 1829, the first Welland Canal was operational, although work continued on it until 1931 to reduce the number of locks and to enlarge its depth in order to facilitate the quick movement of larger ships through the canal. A writer of the time commented on the appeal of the area:

No work in Europe or America will bear comparison with its usefulness. In touching upon the mighty results which must soon follow its completion, the truth will assume the appearance of the most extravagant exaggeration, to those who do not make themselves acquainted with the singular geographical position of North America. The great inland seas above the Falls of Niagara, containing more than half the fresh water upon this planet — bounded by upwards of 400,000 square miles of as fertile land as can be found on the globe, and exceeding in length of coast, five thousand miles. These seas, affording the most beautiful and commodious means of internal communication ever beheld, on a scale which science and human labour or the treasures of a world cannot rival — can be approached by ships, only through the Welland Canal, with which in point of usefulness, no other work of the kind in Europe or Asia, ancient or modern will bear any comparison.

By 1835 St. Catharines was known as one of the terminals of the Underground Railroad. Canadian slavery had been abolished since August 1, 1834, and Upper Canada in the 1850s was still part of the British Empire. One of the symbols of the British monarchy is a lion, so when Harriet would speak of being under the "lion's paw" it meant to be under the protection of British authority. It was understood that Queen Victoria, her government, and her armies would protect the freedom of self-emancipated people. While few records exist, it is likely that Harriet Tubman supported herself in much the same way she did in Philadelphia or Cape May. She likely worked as a housekeeper, cook, or laundress while in St. Catharines, which is in keeping with the types of jobs that other black women would have had. Service positions were occupations that many blacks and lower class whites were relegated to; only a few were able to break into businesses of their own. But these were people seeking to survive, and any respectable means of earning money for their survival would be acceptable. These were also the types of jobs that would allow Harriet to have the flexibility to begin and quit as she wished, making it easy to leave her job and carry out other rescue missions in the south. Harriet never asked for anything for herself, but if her wages did not supply her with enough money for the care of the many fugitives or self-emancipated people she had living with her, she might have turned to others for assistance.

Black men, and others, found work on the Welland Canal. The Canal itself helped industries develop that needed labourers — grist mills, flour mills, salt springs, foundries, machine shops, saw mills, woollen factories, distilleries, newspapers, ship yards, and dry docks — and blacks were called in to patrol the Welland Canal to keep the peace between Catholic and Protestant workers of Irish ancestry. The Canal provided cheap and plentiful power for the mills and manufacturing that developed. The security role for blacks was an extension of their military service in the Colored Corps, and continued until the Canal was almost complete and did not need so many workers. The Colored Corps had a role in customs and excise problems as they worked to end smuggling from the United States, and they would later work on road construction.

St. Catharines had the "look of prosperity and business capa-
bilities, far in advance of its size and appearance." It was a booming
industrial town that needed and welcomed workers. Most of the
American- or Canadian-born blacks who appeared in the Canada
census by 1861 were self-supporting through working in St.
Catharines as labourers, although some were skilled tradespeople
such as masons, coopers, barbers, hairdressers, shoemakers, bar-
tenders, boat drivers, or carpenters. Some men or women lived
in the homes of wealthier whites and worked as servants, such as
cooks, housekeepers, or care givers. Others were self-sufficient
through farming. One visitor to the area noted:

> Scattered around, and within five miles, are large
> numbers of [black] farmers, many of whom have
> become wealthy since escaping into Canada.
> Going into the market on Saturday morning, I
> counted 37 colored persons selling their com-
> modities, consisting of ducks, chickens, eggs,
> butter, cheese, hams, bacon, vegetables and
> fruits of all kind.

For many, St. Catharines's prosperity made it a likely place to
settle in for good, but others moved on to cities serviced by the
Canal, Toronto, smaller towns, and, by the end of the Civil War,
back to the United States to try to reconnect with family. Blacks
tended to live close to each other because they faced similar economic and social barriers, and their homes tended to be on the
outskirts of the city on land that was not as desirable at the time.
Because they lived close together, churches and schools grew
to meet their needs as a community. African Canadians were
sometimes settled together, as with the military, or they were

attracted to areas where there was tolerance for their presence or because of reasonable rates. The St. Catharines black community lived primarily in the area bounded by North, Geneva, Welland, and Williams Streets. St. Catharines blacks were within this area because Oliver Phelphs and William Hamilton Merritt owned a large tract of land bordering on North Street. In 1835, African Canadians were encouraged to buy land there because they could obtain favourable terms to purchase the land, including long leases. It seems that in some cases payments were not made by the black residents if they were unable to manage the expense and that interest was not charged. Merritt also donated a lot of land for the building of a church and meeting hall for the black community along the North Street area.

William Hamilton Merritt was the child of former American residents who had fought on the side of the British during the American War of Independence. Not able to remain in the newly independent country, the Merritts initially moved to New Brunswick and then settled in the area now known as St. Catharines. William became a successful businessman and politician, and he was the visionary of the Welland Canal and the Niagara Suspension Bridge. Additionally, as his abolitionist views supported the growing numbers of enslaved African Americans entering St. Catharines as free people, understanding the oppression they had experienced in slavery.

> The Hon. Mr. Merritt spoke in terms of condemnation of the institution, and favorably of the conduct of the refugee slaves in this part of Canada, and recommended that something practical be done in their favor.
>
> — *St. Catharines Standard*, April 1852

Merritt's provision of land to what is now the Salem Chapel British Methodist Episcopal Church may have cost about 1 dollar (5 shillings at the time). Merritt also worked to establish the Fugitive Slave Friends Society to proactively seek clothing, books, and funds to support the expanding community of new free black people.

Oliver Phelps was from Connecticut where he had worked as a contractor. He immigrated to St. Catharines and experienced great wealth through his business acumen — investing and profiting from investment in trade industries. He is responsible for naming both Geneva and Court Streets in the area of town where he, along with William Hamilton Merritt, owned most of the land.

St. Catharines was a beautiful centre with a mild climate that produced plenty of food and work through the many orchards and gardens. The Welland Canal and the abundant water power of the region made navigation central to the economy and helped in the development of goods and services. St. Catharines was close to other centres and is noted as having a good public spirit. The St. Catharines black community was viewed in a positive light. According to Mary Ann Shadd, the first black woman publisher/newspaper person in North America:

> During my stay at St. Catharines I had frequent opportunities of examining the general improvements of the place and was in no way more gratified than when viewing the snug homesteads of the colored people. Messrs. Maddern, Young, Lindsay and others are adding largely by their enterprise to the beauty of

the place. Their success is a standing refutation to the falsehood that begging is needed for the fugitives of St. Catharines.

Another writer, William Wells Brown, describes the "coloured settlement" as follows:

> The colored settlement is a hamlet, situated on the outskirts of the village, and contains about 100 houses, 40 of which lie on North Street, the Broadway of the place. The houses are chiefly cottages, with from 3 to 6 rooms, and on lots of land nearly a quarter of an acre each. Most of the dwellings are wood-colored, only a few of them having been painted or whitewashed. Each family has a good garden, well-filled with vegetables, ducks, chickens, and a pig-pen, with at least one fat grunter getting ready for Christmas. The houses with the lots upon which they stand, are worth upon average $500 each. Some of them have devoted a small part of the garden to the growth of the tobacco plant, which seems to do well. Entering North Street at the lower end, I was struck with surprise at the great number of children in the street.... The houses in the settlement are all owned by their occupants, and from inquiry I learned that the people generally were free from debt. Out of the eight hundred in St. Catharines, about seven hundred of them are fugitive slaves. I met one old lady who escaped at the advanced age

of eighty-five years — she is now *one hundred and four*. Among them I found seventeen carpenters, four blacksmiths, six coopers, and five shoemakers. Two omnibuses and two hacks are driven by colored men. Not long since, a slave run away from Virginia, came here, and settled down; a few months after, his master "broke down," cheated his creditors, escaped to Canada, came and settled by the side of his former chattel. Their families borrow and lend now, upon terms of perfect equality.

As St. Catharines was becoming more noted as a terminus on the Underground Railroad, the Secretary of State for Canada, Henry Clay, stated in 1828 that he viewed "the escape of slaves as a growing evil which menaces the peaceful relations between the United States and Canada." He hoped to see an extradition treaty to return runaways to their owners — this even after black people had been invited to join the side of the British and be granted their freedom for their loyalty. However, just as there were anti-slavery sympathizers among the residents of St. Catharines, there were also residents and visitors alike who felt the correct position for an African was in service at the least or in bondage at the most.

While black Canadians helped in the building of at least one of the resort spas — the Welland House, renowned for its bathhouse with healthful saline and mineral spring waters, and worked as waiters — they were denied service because they were black. Neighbouring towns also excluded them from renting hotel rooms. In one case, a black minister and his wife travelling through Drummondville and Niagara Falls from Brantford, on their way to Buffalo, were refused accommodation during a snowstorm in January 1852. Wealthy (white) American tourists or political refugees from the States, who had little difficulty finding accommodation, would come in and pay $2 to $3 dollars a day and often reside at the spas for the season from April to October. In 1854, blacks were outraged that the public buses of the St. Catharines House and the American Hotel would not carry them. Two black ministers of the AME Church were among those denied transportation. At a meeting called at the BME Church at Geneva and North on August 4, a plan of action was developed by the ministers, some waiters of the hotels owning the buses, and other residents. The head waiter of the American Hotel threatened to quit his job in protest, followed by support from a St. Catharines House waiter, who stated that "insults and outrages heaped on others, on account of prejudice (are the same as if) … committed against himself." It was decided at that community meeting:

> *Resolved,* That in this glorious land of Freedom, and under this equitable and powerful Government, man is man, without respect to the colour of his skin, and that we, as men, will not submit to degrading terms of service, nor see our brethren treated with indignity by public conveyances, or excluded therefrom, without showing a manly spirit of resentment. *Resolved,* That, as waiters, at the public hotels, of St. Catharines, we will not continue in the service of our present employers, unless, in the management of their conveyances, they henceforth treat ourselves and our people with the respect and civility, to which

we are entitled, as men. With this expression of
affirmation and solidarity and with the support
of influential members of the community also
threatening to boycott these establishments, the
hotels changed their policies.

The building of the Welland House provided jobs for black
people in the 1800s. The Welland House and the other spa hotels
connected to natural hot water springs or therapeutic waters —
such as The Springbank or the Stephenson House — developed
around the local salt springs which were thought to have healing
powers. Affluent people from around the world were attracted
by these springs, especially the United States, and they flocked to
St. Catharines for rest and relaxation. Guests of the spas included
Mary Todd Lincoln (the widow of Abraham Lincoln), the aunt
of Robert E. Lee, various spies, and tourists from the American
South who travelled with their enslaved black staff. Because
the white guests from the south expected the black people in St.
Catharines should be subservient but they were not, the guests
forced the hotel owners to exclude black people from equal
access to the hotels, giving rise to racial conflict. Today the spas
are closed and only the structure of the Welland House remains.

Anthony Burns became a resident of St. Catharines after an
arduous course of events and likely was convinced that Canada
was indeed the Promised Land.

Born a slave in Virginia on May 31, 1834, Burns was owned
by Colonel Charles Suttle. Suttle hired him out to work for others, and Burns was able to escape — finally ending up in Boston.
On May 24, 1854, he was arrested in Boston under the terms

of the *Fugitive Slave Act*. Following a town meeting in support of Burns, there was a riot in which several people were injured and one was killed. Burns was put on trial on June 2, and it was ruled that he had to be sent back to Colonel Suttle. Because of the anger of the citizens of Boston, Burns was escorted out of the city by twenty-two state militia to prevent any crowd violence. Over 50,000 people lined the street to protest the decision and witness his transfer back to Suttle.

Burns was returned to Virginia where he was severely beaten and confined to a cage for months by Suttle. He was later sold to a plantation in North Carolina. Finally members of the Boston church he had attended purchased him and a matron financed his education at Oberlin College in Ohio as a student of religious studies. By 1860, Burns had moved to St. Catharines, serving as the pastor of Zion Baptist Church on Geneva Street. He died on July 27, 1862, at the age of twenty-eight, and was buried at Victoria Lawn Cemetery in St. Catharines. His courage and dedication have been commemorated with a plaque — he was the last enslaved person to be captured in Massachusetts.

Courtesy of the Library of Congress.

After rescue, kidnapped blacks tell their story.

* * *

During her very first winter in St. Catharines, in December 1851, Harriet conducted a group of eleven people on the UGRR that included her brother and his wife.

> They earned their bread by chopping wood in the snows of a Canadian forest; they were frost-bitten, hungry and naked. Harriet was their good angel. She kept house for her brother, and the poor creatures boarded with her. She worked for them, begged for them, and carried them by the help of God through the hard winter.

St. Catharines was a significant centre for the reception of black people on the Underground Railroad, with an African-Canadian population of over 1,000 out of a total population of about 7,000. Blacks primarily lived around the Geneva, Niagara, Cherry and Williams Street area, although some lived in the homes where they were employed throughout St. Catharines or in nearby farming areas. From the assessment records of St. Catharines, it was learned that Harriet rented a house for herself and for the reception of refugees on Lot 11, North Street, near the corner of Geneva. It was close to what is believed to be her house of worship, now called the British Methodist Episcopal Church of Canada, Salem Chapel, at 92 Geneva Street, which still serves the needs of the present-day community. She also had a connection to the AME Zion Church.

Financial assistance, in addition to what Harriet earned, came from many sources, including the American Missionary Society and the Anti-Slavery Society of Canada, presided over by Dr. Michael Willis of the University of Toronto. Ideological support came through George Brown, an abolitionist and owner of the Toronto newspaper, the *Globe and Mail*. Anti-slavery support was very high in Toronto and was shared by some local, influential people. Black people settled throughout Canada, especially in Ontario and the Maritime provinces, but within Ontario Harriet preferred St. Catharines. Why did Harriet Tubman prefer St. Catharines to other Canadian cities? Clearly the booming economy of the 1850s made it relatively easy to make a living, but the acts of anti-black racism detracted from this potential prosperity and security. Since Harriet and her charges were fresh from plantation-style experiences she may have found more positive than negative in the St. Catharines community. Its distance from the American border suited her, it was inland enough to not be too attractive to bounty hunters and it meant that her Underground Railroad trips were somewhat brief within Canadian territory.

The industrial growth in the area had ensured that former enslaved Africans would be able to find a means of supporting themselves. But Harriet liked to have a main contact in each town she passed through, someone whom she felt she could trust completely, someone who could provide unconditional support to herself and to her people, and in St. Catharines she found Reverend Hiram Wilson. Born in New Hampshire, Hiram Wilson had settled in Toronto after completing his religious studies. Acting as an agent for the American Anti-Slavery Society, he travelled throughout Ontario and established ten schools. He worked with Josiah Henson to establish the British North America Institute in Dresden. However, he was saddened by the loss of his wife and the concerns over the financial management of the Dresden scheme. As he was about to return to the United States, the passing of the 1850 *Fugitive Slave Act* made him consider remaining in Canada to assist the large numbers of fugitives entering the country.

> I was almost in despair of continuing in Canada & thought seriously of seeking some other field & in fact had packed up my effects at Dawn to facilitate removal before we made our journey to the East in September thinking then of planting ourselves in the West but after the infamous fugitive Bill had passed & became a law I resolved to return & continue in Canada, at this most fearful crisis with the colored people.

He settled in St. Catharines, received financial support from the American Missionary Association, operated a fugitive relief station, and set up a number of schools with teachers who he knew from Oberlin College. He was one of the four whites to have attended the North American Convention, and with others he represented St. Catharines.

> I am to guard the Niagara Frontier and do all that can reasonably be done in this section of Canada for the welfare of the Refugees who are here quite numeral are rapidly increasing.
> We are in the midst of an enterprising village of 4000 inhabitants but 14 miles from Niagara falls 11 miles from Queenston 12 [miles] from Niagara 3 [miles] from Lake Ontario 34 [miles] from Buffalo.

He was a main contact for Harriet Tubman in St. Catharines and was active as an abolitionist and a refugee supporter. In fact, upon her initial arrival she may have met him, or he may have made arrangements for her to be hosted by his supportive wife at Bethel Chapel, AME Church, a log building on North Street. It later became a BME Church. Wilson indicated that he was in New York State in December of 1851 — when Tubman made her journey with eleven others — and did not return to St. Catharines until New Years Day, which would have been January 1, 1852. He does not mention travelling with a band of freedom seekers — is this when Tubman arrived, or was it later? Was he just being overly cautious, or had he yet to realize the significance of his new arrivals? A letter Wilson wrote states:

> St. Catharines C.W
> Dear Brother Hill Feb. 5th 1852
>
> Some time having elapsed since I have commu-
> nicated I take the liberty to make known to you
> something of our circumstances the foremost
> winter. I spent the latter part of Dec. in the state
> of N.Y making Utica the farthest point of travel
> Returned to my family on New Years day I have
> been at home ...

In his many letters written to fellow classmates from Oberlin, members of the American Anti-Slavery Society, or potential sponsors, he is careful to not reveal too many details of his efforts to aid refugee slaves. While Tubman was among the most famous of his associates, he rarely made full mention of her by name. Granted, this was early in her "career" as a freedom leader. Such was the ongoing issue connected to interacting with "fugitive slaves," even when they were on free soil.

Wilson needed to be able to travel freely to solicit funds, and his concern for undermining the effectiveness of the UGRR, should his letters have been intercepted, was clear. What is also clear was the difficulty in finding the means to provide the type of assistance that the new arrivals required. In this letter written soon after Harriet Tubman and her first group arrived in St. Catharines, one can see how dedicated Wilson was in trying to assist them with their crucial settlement issues, namely food and fuel:

> We have had some intensively cold weather this winter in this quarter, colder than has been known for many years thermometer having fallen down to 15 [degrees] below zero. It has been very hard on the poor.
>
> A considerable number of colored families had come over from the state of New York for protection late in Autumn & not having opportunity to prepare for winter they have suffered to some extent and but for over timely & [illegible] exertions in their behalf they would have been many greatly sufferers[.]
>
> From the first of [January] till about 10 days ago I was inexpertly on the move for the purpose of [illegible] living the destitute. Some were entirely out of provisions & had no means of obtaining any Some destitute of both food & fuel. My means were soon exhausted & to prevent people from suffering I have made the best

use I could of credit and owe now [invalued?] to a considerable amount in behalf of others.

In view of the destroyed condition of the people & my own [liabilities] incurred in releasing them I have made appeals to friends in New York and at the last which may meet with a response if we wait patiently but I do not expect much....

Wilson assisted those in need and harnessed the resources of individuals who could inspire the new Canadians — people like Jermain Loguen. Loguen was an ordained AME Zion minister who came to St. Catharines to avoid being arrested in Syracuse, New York, for his part in helping a slave escape. A self-freed man himself, Loguen worked not only with the church, but also with the Underground Railroad movement in New York. His own experiences and his expertise with fugitives made him a helpful addition to the abolition group in St. Catharines. He worked with Reverend Hiram Wilson providing for their needs.

Another St. Catharines black resident, Nelson Countee, a signor of the hotel petition, entered Canada in the 1840s and the AME ministry in 1844. He also was involved in fugitive relief.

As previously mentioned, William Hamilton Merritt, MP, was key in setting the tone in St. Catharines. He was born in Bedford, West Chester County, New York, on July 3, 1793. Merritt's father was a United Empire Loyalist and a military man who served with a unit commanded by Colonel John Graves Simcoe. Upon learning of Simcoe's new appointment as Lieutenant Governor of Upper Canada (now Ontario), he visited his old friend in Niagara and moved his family to Canada when William was three years old. Merritt's father was appointed sheriff of the Niagara district and purchased land on Twelve Mile Creek — the area that became known as Merriton. His father was also credited with promoting the healthful qualities of the springs in St. Catharines.

As a young man, William Merritt fought in the War of 1812 and following the war he opened a general store, sawmill, and flour mill on the site of present-day St. Catharines. He also purchased some three hundred acres of land nearby. He promoted the transportation system to enhance commerce between Ontario and New York, including construction of the Welland Canal, which saw the first boats through the canal on October 24, 1829.

By 1832 he was elected to the legislature of Upper Canada and continued his interest in transportation facilities between the two countries. In the 1840s, he developed the concept of the Niagara Suspension Bridge, which was completed by 1849 and used by escaping enslaved Africans in the following years. He died on July 5, 1864.

The idea for a land connection between southern Ontario and Upper New York came from Merritt's success in building the Welland Canal and his interest in improving trade between the two countries. He felt that a land route would allow carriages access to the markets of St. Catharines, encourage more business on both sides of the border, and attract tourists for the mineral spring spas. Merritt used his experience as a financial agent for the Welland Canal Company to start the project.

A community called Suspension Bridge grew up near Drummondville at the north end of Niagara Falls, Ontario, and a similar settlement on the American side had the same name. Later the community referred to as Suspension Bridge became known as Niagara Falls, and today Bridge Street marks the location of the centre of this community in Ontario. In 1849 the building of the suspension bridge was complete, with two levels combining a train bridge with a motor way, one over the other.

It was ideal for freedom seekers — perhaps there would be no guard posted at the entrance, or the guard would just look the other way. It is known that on at least one occasion, Harriet Tubman took an actual train ride across the suspension bridge with her human "cargo," before making their way into St. Catharines.

8

Taking the Railroad into Canada

William Hamilton Merritt was called "the Father of Canadian Transportation" for his work on the Welland Canal, and he was also a member of the Refugee Slaves' Friends Society (RSFS) formed in 1852. This organization offered financial, employment, and housing assistance to fugitives, and many local blacks, including Harriet Tubman, were involved with this organization. The first mayor of St. Catharines, Elias Smith Adams, was one of the founders of the RSFS.

In addition to providing immediate relief to "fugitives," the RSFS worked to send the now free blacks on to Toronto. Many of the surnames of African Canadians who settled for a time in St. Catharines as reflected in the 1861 census, spread throughout the area and continue among contemporary blacks in Ontario today. Names like Ball, Hollingsworth, Miles, and Jackson exist among Toronto families which have long roots in Canada. Other families documented in the 1861 census, such as Johnson, Jones,

Miller, Sheffield, and Stewart, have descendants living in St. Catharines, Hamilton, Brantford, Cayuga, Collingwood, Owen Sound, Windsor, and London, Ontario. The following is an 1899 death notice about a black man who settled in Brantford, Ontario. Note his surname and the surnames of his pallbearers — more survivors of the UGRR.

> Ex Slave Dead
> Peter Johnson Passed Away — Attacked with Blood-Hounds
>
> Peter Johnson aged 78 died Saturday at the hospital. He was born in slavery on a southern plantation, and after reaching maturity made a dash for liberty. He was tracked with blood-hounds, but succeeded in effecting his escape and finally reaching British soil by way of "the underground railroad."
> Johnson lived in Brantford since 1857 and was respected as a hardworking capable citizen. He is buried at Mt. Hope Cemetery. Pallbearers were Messrs. John S. Jones, Thomas Snowden, Nocholas MGormas, Charles Walker, Joseph Purly and Stephen Brown.

— The *Brantford Expositor*, June 26, 1899

From the entry point at Niagara and their stay in St. Catharines, many travelled further from the border in search of jobs, their own land, or family members. Hamilton was attractive at the time since people could get their start in the ship-building industry there. The need to fell the forests of black walnut, oak, and ash provided employment for black people in "Little Africa" — what towns heavily populated with fugitive slaves were called — until the wood reserves were exhausted.

Harriet Tubman remained in St. Catharines and was one of the black people who was an active member of the interracial RSFS. She was also an executive of the Fugitive Aid Society (FAS) in 1861. She is credited with being the reason for the success of the FAS. Harriet's work in conducting people from the land of bondage to the land of freedom contributed to the role St. Catharines' importance with the UGRR. She was obviously interested in making sure that all of "her people" were going to get the start-up or ad hoc assistance they would need.

Harriet's fourth trip on the Underground Railroad was a turning point for her. She had to travel further than she was used to, so she came to Canada first and began to work with other Underground Railroad "staff" to ensure the safety of her passengers. Frederick Douglass, abolitionist, orator, and a self-emancipated man, gave freedom seekers shelter in his Rochester home; William Still kept records of blacks who needed assistance in order to potentially reunite families, including his own, in Philadelphia; Thomas Garrett routinely escorted passengers across the Christiana River.

Both Still and Garrett documented the work of Harriet Tubman, indicating that she made four trips by 1851 and at least eight more trips by 1856. Harriet claimed to have made nineteen or more trips before the Civil War, probably eleven of those trips beginning and ending in St. Catharines. On one rescue mission, Harriet stopped at what had been the home of a free black to obtain food, shelter, and other assistance. Instead, the home was now occupied by a white man who told Harriet that the previous resident had to leave because he was harbouring

runaway slaves. Harriet quickly joined her hidden passengers
and moved them to a swamp to avoid detection. She prayed all
day, and by dusk a Quaker walked to the edge of the swamp
and said that his barn had a wagon with provisions that they
could use. This showed the effectiveness of the Underground
Railroad communications. Abolitionists were watching for her
party, which reinforced Harriet's faith. By 1854, a formal connection with Garrett ensured that other freedom seekers would
not get stranded at this point in their flight.

Harriet felt that something was wrong in Bucktown, and
this was confirmed through Underground Railroad communication. Someone who was secretly working with the Underground
Railroad passed a message on to someone who could give it to
Harriet. Harriet learned that her brothers, Benjamin, Henry, and
Robert, were to be sold on December 26, 1854. She arranged for a
coded letter to be sent to a literate free black named Jacob Jackson
who knew her family. Jackson was under suspicion of helping
slaves escape, so to protect the letter writer and the family she
wished to rescue, Harriet needed to find an indirect method of
communicating her intentions. The letter was "signed" by Jacob
Jackson's adopted free son, who lived in the north, William Henry
Jackson. Jackson's letter was first read by his employer (even free
blacks could not expect privacy or respect for their mail) who
did not understand the meaning of the letter, even after he con-
sulted others in the community. Finally, Jackson himself was
summoned and given his own mail to read. It stated in part:

> Read my letter to the old folks, and give my love
> to them, and tell my brothers to be always watch-
> ing unto prayer, and when the good ship of Zion
> comes along, to be ready to step on board.

Jackson, having no parents or brothers, pretended he did not understand it when questioned by his white overseer, but he immediately told Harriet's brothers to get ready because Harriet was coming to get them. On Christmas Eve, Harriet met her brothers near Ben and Rit's cabin with three other freedom seekers: John Chase, Peter Jackson, and Jane Kane. They knew they could not expect Rit to be quiet if she knew that Harriet was there — she would be too excited! They did, however, let Ben know that they were leaving, and he discreetly brought food to the group as they hid during the day. He covered his eyes with a bandanna so that he would truthfully be able to say, when questioned by his owner, that he had not "seen" his sons. He knew he would be interrogated and he wanted to be ready. After travelling the 100 miles to Wilmington, they were assisted by Garrett. They arrived in St. Catharines in early 1855.

A portrait of Frederick Douglass, included as one of the "Heroes of the Colored Race."

Harriet was quoted in an 1858 St. Catharines newspaper, saying, "I wouldn't trust Uncle Sam with my people no longer.... I brought 'em all clar off to Canada." But Harriet and others were more like exiles than immigrants — they were forced to leave the land of their birth because of the severity of southern slavery and the risks of remaining in the north. Harriet longed for the familiar aspects of her life, but could not have the freedom she desired in the country she was from. While in St. Catharines she said, "[We are] in a foreign country among strangers. We would rather stay in our native land, if we could be as free there as we are here."

Passengers on the Underground Railroad often wore disguises to further throw off any suspicion. Sometimes women dressed as men, or a light-coloured slave might assume the role of a slave owner in order to travel with other darker-coloured freedom seekers. If someone was light skinned, they might be darkened. Fancy outfits belonging to free blacks might be borrowed to give the freedom seeker wearing the clothes the look of an affluent person. There were instances when a disguise might not have been enough to escape the reach of a search party, and individuals are known to have been hidden away until the intensity of the search seemed to be over, sometimes for months, before they could continue on their journey to freedom. According to oral history from descendants, particularly the late Marlene Wilkins, Harriet often wore several layers of clothing, especially pantaloons, in order to protect herself from the cold, perhaps to appear heavier, but also to protect herself from the tracking dogs. If a dog were to chase Harriet as she was travelling with a party of escaping slaves, and if it were to bite her, the dog would only be left with her clothing. She was concerned that these hounds not have the opportunity to taste her blood since she would then not be able to successfully conduct on the Underground Railroad — they would track her to death.

Harriet may have appeared as a simple old woman with her noisy chickens, as a slave travelling further south for her assumed master, or just as one of the many slaves in the area. Her demeanour and the way she carried herself were also important in her success — she would not have allowed herself to outwardly seem afraid or worried as her papers were being checked or as someone who could identify her came near. Her belief in the good of her cause gave her the resources to deal with obstacles. But it took more than Harriet Tubman's confidence — she made all the necessary arrangements that she could in advance of her departure. Her bag carried the essentials for her trip: from the sharpened clam shells for protection or influence through to the tranquillizer to quiet babies. She knew what safe houses she was aiming to reach and where there would be food for her group. She had a plan for extra clothing for disguises or warmth and knew where she could find the "stockholders" of the UGRR — those who would provide her with funds or actual train tickets. She was the master of communications and worked her trusted and potential connections to the best of her ability.

In order to get to Canada, Harriet did not always follow the same route, and sometimes she actually travelled south in order to avoid suspicion if she felt she had been identified. She might pre-arrange to meet her group at the beginning of the month or during a new moon, as the lack of light would make the group more difficult to see. If enough money was available, passage would be purchased on the Philadelphia, Wilmington, and Baltimore Railroads, or water routes and canal trenches could also be utilized. Harriet and her party would primarily be using their own two feet, and often wore out more than one pair of shoes on their escape. She is known to have used stations in Camden, Dover, Blackbird, Middleton, New Castle, Wilmington, Laurel, Milford, Millsborough, Concord, Seaford, Smyma, and Delaware City. She also used stations in Pennsylvania and New York, including Syracuse, Auburn, Rochester, and Niagara Falls.

Harriet is known to have crossed on the actual railroad suspension bridge from Niagara Falls, New York, into Niagara Falls, Ontario, which has been documented at least once. Being such a well patrolled site, and given that Harriet used many routes to transport her human cargo, it is unlikely that she made the suspension bridge her only point of entry into Canada. The Niagara River, away from the falls, is rather narrow, and many UGRR stations existed all along the shores of Lake Ontario and Lake Erie. Some accounts indicate that UGRR crossings included Astibula and Port Albino, sites closer to the Fort Erie/Buffalo area. There was also a well-organized ferry crossing between Buffalo, New York, and Fort Erie, Ontario, which could have been used or that provided a route to follow. The Native people crossed the river on rafts at several points that might have been used by freedom seekers working with indigenous people. Harriet and other determined people would have to assess their situations and decide whether to try a familiar or new crossing point.

Because freedom seekers felt protected in her company and because Harriet had been able to avoid recapture or death, she came to be referred to as "Moses," freeing her people, and she earned the respect of whites working in the abolition movement. Thomas Garrett said of her, "If she had been a white woman, she would have been heralded as the greatest woman of her age." Her charm and perseverance also made her credible and gained her allies from among the elite in society. The spiritual song "Go Down Moses" could not be sung by blacks in the south for fear of exposing Harriet's nickname, but it is a beautiful song full of the indignation of enslaved people:

> Oh go down, Moses,
> Way down in Egypt's land.
> Tell old Pharaoh,
> Let my people go.

> Oh Pharaoh said he would go cross,
> Let my people go,
> And don't get lost in de wilderness,
> Let my people go.

> Oh go down Moses,
> Way down in Egypt's land.
> Tell old Pharaoh,
> Let my people go.

> You may hinder me here, but you can't up dere,
> Let my people go,
> He sits in de Hebben and answers prayer,
> Let my people go.

A famous photo of Harriet Tubman. Known as the "Moses of Her People," she served the Union Army as a nurse, scout, and a spy during the Civil War.

Oh go down Moses,
Way down in Egypt's land.
Tell old Pharaoh,
Let my people go.

Others feel that Harriet's success in rescuing enslaved people may have inspired the spiritual "Swing Low, Sweet Chariot." The chorus suggests that freedom will be yours if you get on board:

Swing low, sweet chariot
Coming for to carry me home.
Swing low, sweet chariot,
Coming for to carry me home.

Harriet had a pattern of working to earn enough money to finance travel into slave states during the summer months, followed by attempting rescues in the fall; working during the winter and rescuing in the spring. In November 1856, Harriet returned to the Bucktown area to bring another group to the north. One member of her group was Josiah Bailey who had cost his new owner $1,000 down and $1,000 to be paid later. To learn respect for his new owner, despite being a loyal worker without a behaviour problem, Josiah was flogged on the very first day of the new ownership arrangement. Consequently, Josiah decided to run, joining Bill, Peter Pennington, Eliza Nokey, and one other on board Harriet's train. A reward of $1,500 was offered for Josiah's return, $800 for Peter, $300 for Bill, and $1,200 for Harriet Tubman. The reward for Harriet was higher than the others because of the significant losses she had caused slave owners in the area.

By June 1859, the Society of Slaveholders decided at their nationwide convention that there should be insurance policies to protect the slaveholders against the loss of their "property" through slaves escaping. This Society also offered a reward of $40,000 (equivalent to more than half a million dollars in current dollars) for the capture of Harriet Tubman. Harriet Tubman was one of the most wanted people in the United States because of her success in conducting people to freedom. The number of people in her party varied from a small group of three up to a group of thirty-nine. Discipline was very important to the success of the rescues. On one rescue mission, Harriet hid in the woods with her passengers and watched as her pursuers stood guard over a well-travelled road. Harriet would later say, "And how we laughed: We was de fools, and dey the wise men; but we wasn't fools enough to go down de high road in de broad daylight."

Harriet learned that her parents were suspected of having assisted with the escape of some "fugitive" slaves and were likely to be arrested. She had waited to rescue them because she knew that they would probably not be sold further south because they would not earn much money on the auction block now that they were so old. With money from the New York Anti-Slavery office, Harriet went to Maryland and made a horse-drawn vehicle out of the remnants of an old buggy, boards, wheels, and a harness out of straw. Her frail parents were thus able to ride all night out of the Bucktown area with some of the belongings they did not want to part with; Rit prized her feather bedtick (comforter) and Ben wanted to keep his broadaxe and other tools. In southern Delaware, Harriet was able to board a train to Wilmington, where Garrett gave Harriet enough money to buy their train passage to Canada. Harriet now had freed all of her family members except for one sister and her children.

Due to the increasing risk to Harriet because of the growing concerns between the north and south regarding slave ownership, Harriet was advised not to attempt any more rescues. Upon making themselves free, former slaves sometimes gave themselves new names in order to conceal their identities in case a bounty hunter came by. Harriet's brothers gave themselves the name "Stewart," perhaps after a shipbuilder in the Bucktown area, or after a reasonable overseer. Another well known "Steward" in the Rochester, New York, area may have inspired their selection of this surname. As a distinguished gentleman, Austin Steward was a prominent social and religious leader of the black community who spoke out on issues such as the passing of the *Fugitive Slave Act*. He had worked for a time in Canada, so his name would have been recognized by members of the black community north of the border too.

Often former slaves gave themselves new names that reflected their new status as self-emancipated people. The surname "Freeman" was often assumed. Slaves would name themselves after political figures who had been supportive of anti-slavery measures, or they would assume names that seemed usual unlike the single, sometimes Biblical names they had been assigned during slavery. Someone known as "Cicero" in Virginia might have become Charles Johnson in Philadelphia and possibly John Freeman in Canada. Some gave themselves names that may have appealed to them. For example, in the 1861 census for St. Catharines, there is a black individual who calls himself Andrew Prettyman!

Blacks entering Canada as fugitives from the repressive American laws or as freedom seekers were cautioned not to tell anyone what their true identity was or to speak about where they were originally from or of the family they had left behind. This was to protect them from bounty hunters and their agents who might be searching for them within Canada. Escape stories might be passed down within families, but the fear of recapture by survivors of the Underground Railroad was very real. Some survivors kept their freedom papers, if they had been granted their freedom, just in case of a problem or an opportunity to return. Sometimes individuals took their escape stories with them to the grave. Similarly, those persons who may have provided ongoing or ad hoc assistance to the Underground Railroad also kept their information to themselves.

Harriet kidnapped the daughter of one of her brothers, or according to oral history, Harriet took an orphaned child, the eight-year-old Margaret, and boarded her with a politician in Auburn, New York, named William Seward. Harriet may have felt that she would be able to ensure a secure and prosperous childhood for Margaret, unlike the experiences that Harriet had at the same age. Some researchers wonder if this Margaret could have been a child of Harriet Tubman, since she took such an interest in her. However, the child is described as being light-skinned, and since neither Harriet nor John are described as being light, the child may or may not have had a family connection. It is possible that Harriet was impregnated by her owner or that the child was actually a niece. The African tradition was to care for the community, so it is also possible that Harriet was acquainted with the child's mother or was asked to care for this child by another enslaved woman wanting to see the best for her.

Towards the end of 1858, Harriet moved her parents to Auburn and made her home there because of Margaret, because of the assistance of Seward — now the Governor of New York and Harriet's strongest supporter — and because Auburn was becoming a centre for abolitionists and the women's suffrage movement. St. Catharines may have ceased to have personal appeal to Harriet because her growing awareness of the enormity of the slave issue made her feel that a major approach in co-operation with sympathetic whites was needed in order to stop slavery and increase tolerance. Harriet may have come to realize that as important as her assistance to a small group might be, it was time to heal the problem by ending slavery. In nineteen life-risking missions, Harriet had rescued, and ensured a livelihood, for over 300 people, but there were thousands of others still suffering. Even if she spent the rest of her life conducting people to safety, she would never be able to free them all.

A movement or political reform that would end slavery had great appeal. William Seward was introduced to Harriet by Frederick Douglass. Seward was a Republican who had opposed the *Fugitive Slave Act*. He was close to winning a presidential election, but his stand on the John Brown issue at Harpers Ferry (a planned slave rebellion) later cost him the win. Seward was able ensure that Harriet was able to bid on the land, and some reports indicate that he loaned Harriet the money to buy property in Auburn which Harriet later repaid with the proceeds from the sale of the Sarah Bradford book, *Scenes in the Life of Harriet Tubman*.

During an 1860 visit to Troy, New York, to see a cousin, Harriet Tubman learned that a slave, Charles Nalle, had been followed by his owner. She postponed her travel to a scheduled anti-slavery meeting in Boston she had been told about by Thomas Gerrit and used her time to alert the community about this man who was already detained.

Over time, people who were slaves began to look like people who were not enslaved. Breeding of Africans and Europeans produced slaves who were half African and half European, who then appeared less and less African-looking as the as the interracial procreation went on. Charles Nalle was a slave who was one-eighth black, as a child of a slave who was one-quarter black and her white master. He ran from his Culpepper County, Virginia, plantation to join his wife. The agent who was sent to find him in Troy, New York, was his half brother. They had the same father, looked alike, but one was a slave and one was free. Nalle was being held in the commissioner's office when Harriet managed to grab him while rousing the crowd outside the building, and she put Nalle onto a waiting boat. On the other side of the river, Nalle was recaptured but freed again by the crowd, and Harriet obtained a ride to safety for him on a passing wagon. Nalle later returned to Troy with money collected from the community to buy his freedom.

Harriet's last known trip on the Underground Railroad may have been the one she made in December 1860 when she tried to find her sister in Maryland. She discovered that her sister had died, so Harriet took seven others with her instead.

9

The Civil War

Without firing a gun, without drawing a sword,
should they make war on us, we could bring the
whole world to our feet ...
What would happen if no cotton was furnished
for three years?...
England would topple headlong and carry the
whole civilized world with her save the South.
No, you dare not to make war on cotton.
No power on the earth dares to make war upon it.
Cotton is King.

— U.S. Senator James Henry Hammond,
owner of Redcliffe Plantation,
in a speech before the United States Senate,
March 4, 1858.

The Civil War in the United States is often seen as being about states' rights, and those rights, particularly for southern planters, clearly rested on the continuation of the enslavement of Africans. Religion played a major role in raising awareness about issues of equality and fair treatment, which challenged slavery, so it was other forms of knowledge, other ideas that people just accepted, that helped to support the continuing interest in enslavement, without guilt and aside from the reality that huge profits could be made by those who operated large plantations.

At this time, the United States' southern cotton plantations produced 80 percent of the cotton used worldwide. What ideas, what concepts could be shared with people, those who had power, those who could vote, those who could ensure that there were not too many changes, to ensure that the "institution" of slavery remained intact? Who could voice those ideas in a broad public sphere? John Henry Hammond is an example of a powerful pro-slavery individual. Hammond was an educated teacher and lawyer, but substantially improved his holdings and his stature upon his marriage to an affluent southern belle. His wife, Catherine, had inherited much property — 7,500 acres of land and 147 enslaved Africans — which then came under his control. The land initially produced $600 in wealth, but increased to $21,000 with his highly controlling measures. He wrote down how enslaved children were to be fed and how they were to be named, what enslaved people were assigned to do, as well as the punishments to be administered to those who opted to flee from his plantations scattered along the Savannah River in South Carolina, including Redcliffe, which today is preserved as a historic site. He was a wealthy and influential South Carolina planter and politician who advocated for maintaining slavery through what he referred to as the Mudsill Theory.

In all social systems there must be a class to do the menial duties, to perform the drudgery of life. That is, a class requiring but a low order of intellect and but little skill. Its requisites are vigor, docility, fidelity. Such a class you must have, or you would not have that other class which leads progress, civilization, and refinement. It constitutes the very mud-sill of society and of political government; and you might as well attempt to build a house in the air, as to build either the one or the other, except on this mud-sill. Fortunately for the South, she found a race adapted to that purpose to her hand. A race inferior to her own, but eminently qualified in temper, in vigor, in docility, in capacity to stand the climate, to answer all her purposes. We use them for our purpose, and call them slaves. We found them slaves by the common "consent of mankind," which, according to Cicero, "*lex naturae est.*" The highest proof of what is Nature's law. We are old-fashioned at the South yet; slave is a word discarded now by "ears polite;" I will not characterize that class at the North by that term; but you have it; it is there; it is everywhere; it is eternal. The Senator from New York said yesterday that the whole world had abolished slavery. Aye, the name, but not the thing; all the powers of the earth cannot abolish that. God only can do it when he repeals the fiat, "the poor ye always have with you;" for the man who lives by daily labor, and scarcely lives at that, and who has to put out his labor in the market, and take the best he can get for it; in short, your whole hireling class of manual laborers and "operatives," as you call them, are essentially slaves. The difference between us is, that our slaves are hired for life and well compensated; there is no starvation, no begging, no want of employment among our people, and not too much employment either. Yours are hired by the day, not cared for, and scantily compensated, which may be proved in the most painful manner, at any hour in any street in any of your large towns. Why, you meet more beggars in one day, in any single street of the city of New York, than you would meet in a lifetime in the whole South. We do not think that whites should be slaves either by law or necessity. Our slaves are black, of another and inferior race. The status in which we have placed them is an elevation. They are elevated from the condition in which God first created them, by being made our slaves. None of that race on the whole face of the globe can be compared with the slaves of the South. They are happy, content, unaspiring, and utterly incapable, from intellectual weakness, ever to give us any trouble by their aspirations. Yours are white, of your own race; you are brothers of one blood. They are your equals in natural endowment of intellect, and they feel galled by their degradation. Our slaves do not vote. We give them no political power. Yours do vote, and, being the majority, they are the depositories of all your political power. If they knew the tremendous secret, that the ballot-box is stronger than "an army with banners," and could combine, where would you be? Your society would be reconstructed, your government overthrown, your property divided, not as they have mistakenly attempted to initiate such proceedings by meeting in parks, with arms in their hands, but by the quiet process of the ballot-box. You have been making war upon us to our very hearthstones. How would you like for us to send lecturers and agitators North, to teach these people this, to aid in combining, and to lead them?

"The 'Mudsill' Theory," by James Henry Hammond. Speech to the U.S. Senate, March 4, 1858.

While this "theory" is attributable to Hammond, it may well have informed and been informed by the Southern gentry, the eventual Confederate South, about what was important, about how to be religiously observant and a slave owner at the same time, and about how important and necessary their efforts were in moving American civilization forward. It was about the need for land, labour, and products, that is, for power to remain in the hands of those who were already powerful — that meant wealthy, white Southern men. With this type of entrenched view, how else but through war could there be a change in the United States at that time?

* * *

John Brown visited St. Catharines with J.W. Longuen in April 1858. John Brown arrived in Chatham on April 29, 1858, to recruit men to end slavery and overthrow the American government. As a white abolitionist, he envisioned surprise attacks being made against plantations from bases in the Appalachians. He felt that slaves freed in this manner would join his trained group, continue attacking plantations, and freeing other slaves until finally setting up a new provisional government. Brown recruited in Chatham, Buxton, Ingersoll, Hamilton, and Toronto and was feeling confident of his support when he met Harriet in St. Catharines. Brown found a black printer in St. Catharines and gave him the provisional constitution to reproduce. Brown asked Harriet to bring as many fugitives to join the pending battle as she could and to be the chief guide to Canada for the many who would want to settle there after the war was waged and won. Brown said that Harriet Tubman was "the most of a man naturally; that [he] ever met with." Brown was greatly impressed with Tubman and referred to her in the male gender as a sign of his admiration for her proven military skill. He advised his son by letter that "General Tubman" had hooked her "whole team" to his cause — Harriett assured Brown of her support. However, when the time came to help, Harriet was unable to come to Brown's assistance due to her illness. Harriet later realized that a recurring dream of hers seemed to mean that Brown and his sons would die in this conflict. Harriet later is known to have said that Brown died because he was too impatient.

With the failure at Harpers Ferry came the death of John Brown, and the heightening of the tensions between slave owners and abolitionists. From *A Voice From Harper's Ferry* written by Osborne Anderson (and edited by Mary Ann Shadd), the only black from Canada to join John Brown on the raid and the only one to survive, we know that John Brown's raid did not go according to plan. A white recruit from Chatham defected and told of the plans, which caused a delay in the raid. Communication problems prevented the maximum number of attackers from getting to the area in time (only twenty were in the raid), whites were being released rather than imprisoned or killed, and they warned others so that by the time John Brown and his party reached their target they were ambushed and hung after a court trial. Their bodies were then fed to pigs instead of being buried.

While there had been at least 250 slave revolts in the United States by the time of Brown's raid, his was one of the first that had white leadership and international support. He raised white fears, forced people to take a stand on slavery, and widened the gap between northern, anti-slavery industrial views and southern, pro-slavery agricultural views. It marked a significant turning point in relations between the Union and the Confederacy which culminated in the American Civil War.

Harriet was too ill to come to John Brown's aid because she had spent the spring of 1859 recruiting throughout New England until the point of exhaustion, one of the only black women to do so. She was recuperating in New Bedford when the raid on Harpers Ferry occurred. As soon as she was able, Harriet Tubman, Frederick Douglass, and three members of the "Secret Six" — the white, northern abolitionists who helped to finance Brown's work — Franklin B. Sanborn, George L. Stearns, and Samuel Grindley Howe, left for Canada after the raid because angry sentiments were so high. Harriet and the others

George Stearns

Gerrit Smith

Frank Sanborn

Thomas Wentworth
Higginson

Theodore Parker

Samuel Gridley Howe

These men were known as the "Secret Six."

were publicly identified as having a connection to John Brown. Despite her absence from the raid itself, Harriet was identified as a co-conspirator through the media and congressional investigation. Many of the few records of the Underground Railroad were destroyed at this time because Underground Railroad workers feared the negative repercussions of the community. But with great foresight, William Still hid his records in a graveyard to preserve them.

As the busiest and the most successful of the conductors on the Underground Railroad, Harriet Tubman managed to bring over 300 people into Canada. Because exact records could not be kept, it is likely that Harriet brought even more captured Africans to safety under the "lion's paw," or British rule. Harriet indicated later in life that she made more than nineteen rescue trips, though some historians doubt this number. However, while the actual number of rescue trips may not be known and is subject to debate, that Harriet Tubman managed even one was sufficient. This was a significant accomplishment given the severe penalties for even reading about abolition in the States, never mind actually motivating and leading people out of bondage. Every time Harriet helped an enslaved person become a free person she was committing a crime, she was causing plantation owners to lose the labour of their slaves, she was disrupting the system, and she was using Canada as a retreat. Every rescue was an anti-slavery statement. And as if Harriet's own personally escorted rescue missions were not successful enough, her reputation inspired others to take the risk of freeing themselves or of going back to their former plantations to lead their families to freedom.

Without the success of the Underground Railroad, there might not have been a Civil War. It heightened the debate between slave-holding interests and those who promoted abolition. Had Canada not been willing to grant the same rights and privileges to blacks as members of other groups, as well as being in such close proximity to the Americans, there would have been no Underground Railroad. In the pioneer society of English-speaking southern Ontario, conditions supported the entry and security of freedom seekers. The climate, economy, and language were similar to that of the northern United States without the constant threat of being recaptured. Mary Ann Shadd, Frederick Douglass, Samuel Ringgold Ward, William Wells Brown, Henry Bibb, and other black intellectuals of the era made a concerted effort to express the positive life experiences of blacks who had made themselves free in Canada. They were concerned about highlighting their successes because pro-slavery interests promoted the notion that people of African descent could not take care of themselves, would be unable to lead wholesome lives, were incapable of learning, and actually *needed* slavery to protect them from themselves since they were inferior creatures. The black abolitionists made it their business to portray the free black community in a positive way since the idea that blacks were not only competent and capable but interested in taking care of themselves was critical to foiling this perception. They travelled throughout the north and the south, speaking wherever they could find an audience, sharing information about how well the blacks in Canada were managing, and how they too could join or support other blacks in getting to Canada.

The free black population of Ontario in particular was raised like a beacon of hope, a successful test case of the potential for free blacks to thrive and contribute. If it could work here, it could work there. It could work anywhere. The successful presence of black peoples in Canada, the holding of the North American Free Men's Convention in Toronto, and Harriet Tubman's work and residence in Canada, combined with the protection of the rights of blacks under the law, was an affront to slave interests and countered their views.

While John Brown's plan for freeing the slaves was unsuccessful, it was an international response to an American situation, since he had recruited in Canada with Harriet Tubman's, and others', support. Harriet was to have rounded up black recruits and motivated them in battle. She was to have played a key role in guiding the African Americans who would be freed by John Brown's raids to Canada. Most of the people who were identified with John Brown were taking refuge in Ontario. Both Harriet and the abolitionists/activists were despised since they were viewed as the main targets who were trying to "subvert" the American way of life. Among the abolitionists and well-placed persons that Tubman knew, was supported by, and worked with were William H. Seward, Louisa May Alcott, Ralph Waldo Emerson, and Susan B Anthony. There were also William Still, and Thomas Garrett, as well as Frederick Douglass. Often Tubman was invited to rest in one of their homes or to bring others to be fuelled for their onward journeys while conducting a group towards Canada.

By April 1861, Harriet was again moved to do what she could to help her people. Through an interview with John Andrews, governor of Massachusetts, and a John Brown supporter, Harriet joined the Union Forces at Hilton Head, then later Beaufort,

South Carolina. She acted as a nurse and became acting head of the hospital. She established a washhouse with the only money she was given during the war: $200. She declined the rations she was entitled to, in deference to her less fortunate neighbours, and spent her evenings making gingerbread, pies, and root beer, which she paid someone to sell for her while she worked during the day.

The lowlands, the Sea Islands near Hilton Head, South Carolina, are remarkably like the terrain of West Africa, where many of the ancestors of the enslaved peoples came from. Here the rice cultivation skills that they arrived with were put to good use. The area was known as the lowlands since they were at sea level. With a tempered climate, and much swamp land, the lowlands were also rather prone to mosquitoes and the related disease of malaria. Since the Africans already had some immunity from their continental upbringing, and since whites had none, plantation owners regularly made arrangements not to be there too often. Slave owners often had more than one plantation or residence, so the enslaved peoples on the Sea Islands were left alone under the direction of their African overseer for weeks, if not months, at a time. This facilitated the retention of African traditions and beliefs and was further fuelled and reinforced by new arrivals, newly enslaved people who had authentic African-isms to share with others.

The people became known as the Gullah People, and had developed their own language — a mix of West African languages, English, and other Creole expressions, as well as their own unique culture and ways of knowing.

By the time the Union Army arrived, they found the Gullah ready to join the fight for their freedom. The southern plantation owners had headed inland indefinitely since they anticipated a naval attack on their coastal properties. The throngs of willing and unsupervised enslaved Africans were included in the Union forces. Harriet may have convinced them to leave their owners to invest their energies with the Union forces. It was Harriet Tubman who challenged herself to work with the Gullah despite what she recognized as a bit of a culture barrier — they spoke differently and had different ways to the people she had grown up with and whom she had come to know — but she found a way to inspire them, to calm them, and to free them.

She worked with Quakers to engage the Gullah in schooling to better prepare them for freedom. By 1862 she was in Beaufort, South Carolina, at the request of Governor Andrew of Massachusetts, and she again acted as a nurse and teacher. In the process, Harriet gained the confidence and trust of the Gullah.

Harriet preferred to be outdoors, so she was pleased to work initially with the First and Second Carolina Regiments as a nurse, then as a spy and a scout. By 1863 Harriet had organized what would be called today an intelligence service, choosing former slaves who knew the terrain to identify food stores or assist in piloting the rivers in preparation for raids. Raids tried to force surrenders from the opposition, gain recruits or raw materials and food, or to destroy property. The information gathered by Harriet made the raids of the Union forces successful. When asked by Colonel Montgomery to see what she could do behind Confederate lines, since the Union still controlled the Sea Islands, Harriet was able to do so. She created a network out of the black men in the area that she could train and trust to see what information they could find out about the activities of the other side, including the ammunition and food stores of the Confederates.

This spy ring, of which she was also an active part, successfully managed to find the information that led to a major victory.

One of the most famous raids was on the Combahee River. The black scouts knew where the mine traps were set in the river and successfully avoided them. Former enslaved field hands piloted gunboats down the river or burned crops and buildings according to Harriet's instructions. Slaves fled from the plantations and were so elated that Harriet tried to calm them through song. Over 750 slaves were taken on board and a Wisconsin journalist credited Harriet as being the one who led the raid, planned the strategy, and carried it out. This made Harriet Tubman the first woman to lead a military assault in American history.

It is likely that the Gullah who were brought into the army had Tubman's guidance to prepare them:

> Col. Montgomery and his gallant band of 800 black soldiers, under the guidance of a black woman, dashed in to the enemies' country ... destroying millions of dollars worth of commissary stores, cotton and lordly dwellings, and striking terror to the heart of rebeldom, brought off near 800 slaves and thousands of dollars worth of property.

— The Boston Commonwealth, July 1863

The military action planned by Tubman on the Combahee River destroyed identified mines and torpedoes in the river, identified Confederate supplies (cotton, rice, potatoes, corn, and farm animals) and disrupted the ability of the Confederates to be replenished. Railroads, bridges, and plantations were destroyed in the wake of this battle. Harriet Tubman not only selected, trained, recruited, and roused the men in preparation for the battle, she also helped to calm the hundreds of enslaved Africans from Confederate-controlled plantations through singing and engaging them in song to calm them down afterwards. And they needed calming. Hundreds of enslaved Africans heard the boat whistle and knew it meant that the gun boats had succeeded in defending them from the Confederate Army. They ran out of their homes, carrying pots of rice, with children hanging around the necks of their parents still digging into the food as they were being carried. Tubman remarked on how many twins she saw and just what a sight it was. So the singing was to calm them down as many of them boarded the boats, paying no mind to their former overseers who were really unable to stop them from leaving. As Tubman indicated:

> I nebber see such a sight. We laughed, an' laughed, an' laughed. Here you'd see a woman wid a pail on her head, rice a smokin' in it jus' as she'd taken it from de fire, young one hangin' on behind, one han' roun' her forehead to hold on, t'other han' diggin' into de rice-pot, eatin' wid all its might; hold of her dress two or three more; down her back a bag wid a pig in it. One woman brought two pigs, a white one an' a black one; we took 'em all on board; named de white pig Beauregard, and de black pig Jeff Davis. Sometimes de women would come wid twins hangin' roun' der necks; 'pears like I nebber see so many twins in my life; bags on der

shoulders, baskets on der heads, and young
ones taggin' behin', all loaded; pigs squealin',
chickens screamin', young ones squallin ...

Because of the way in which smaller boats were sent out to
bring newly freed people on board it was a slow process and
some were fearful that the smaller boats would not return to pick
them up. So it was the excitement of the news, the challenges of
loading, and the relief of the end of the battle that caused people
to be so emotional.

According to General Saxton, in his report on the Combahee
Raid to the Secretary of War Stanton, "This is the only military command in American history wherein a woman, black or
white, led the raid and under whose inspiration it was originated
and conducted."

Harriet continued her service to the Union forces by cooking, doing laundry, and carrying dispatches for units. She served
Colonel Robert Gould Shaw, of the black Fifty-Fourth Regiment
of Massachusetts, his last meal prior to the Fort Wagner battle
in Charleston Harbour, captured in the 1990 film *Glory*. Harriet
described this battle, which ended with the death of 1,500 black
troops that she helped to bury, as follows:

Then we saw de lightening, and that was de
guns; and then we heard de thunder, and that
was de big guns; and then we heard de rain
falling, and that was de drops of blood falling;
and when we came to get in de crops, it was
dead men that we reaped.

Harriet requested a leave of absence in the spring of 1864 and returned to Auburn to rest. At this time she was likely interviewed by Sarah Bradford who produced the closest thing we have to an autobiography of Harriet Tubman. Sarah, a teacher in the Auburn area, befriended Tubman and saw this effort as a means of allowing Tubman to acquire some funds. The first Bradford book, *Scenes in the Life of Harriet Tubman*, published in 1869, brought in about $1,000 to help address Tubman's financial distress. The second publication, *Harriet, the Moses of her People*, released in 1886, was also intended to address Tubman's need for funds.

By the summer of 1864 Harriet was again well enough to travel to Boston, meeting the sixty-seven-year-old Sojourner Truth. Sojourner was an outspoken speaker on women's rights, abolition, and religion. Harriet declined an invitation to join Sojourner at a meeting with President Lincoln because she felt he had done little to free the slaves. Harriet and other abolitionist and black leaders had been shocked when President Abraham Lincoln denied that the goal of the Civil War was to end slavery, and Lincoln had declined to accept blacks in the Union Army until 1863. Volunteers of African descent were allowed to enlist only after pressure from abolitionists and military strategists, and well after the preliminary Emancipation Proclamation giving freedom to slaves in states, which were still embroiled in Civil War conflicts effective January 1, 1863. Harriet did not feel that Lincoln deserved praise for his treatment of people of African descent, feeling that John Brown had done more.

Always ready to serve, Harriet found herself back to tending to wounded soldiers. By 1865, she was acting as the matron of the Fortress Monroe Colored Hospital in Virginia. Deeply dedicated to alleviating suffering, she helped to fundraise for the education of children and freed adults. She also had the care of her parents to deal with, and by 1868 the home that she had was expanded to become the Home for Aged and Indigent Colored People.

Also later in 1865, Harriet agreed to assist Martin Delany in recruiting and training a black military unit drawn from the population of the south. The surrender of General Robert E. Lee, general-in-chief of the Confederate Army, made this unnecessary. But Harriet was willing to work in the government hospital in Fort Munroe, Virginia. Most of the sick had dysentery, severe and painful diarrhea, and with a remedy Harriet had learned from her family or other slaves, they recovered in a day. The herbal medicine she used was derived from roots of the pond lily and wild geranium. Her expertise was needed in Fernadina, Florida, where she next worked. She was appointed "matron" (superintendent) of this hospital after complaining about the conditions there. Harriet, for all her value to the government, still had not received anything more than the original $200 given to her in 1861.

Harriet had a long connection to sickness and healing. As a child, she had become seriously ill while tending swamp traps. It was only her mother's knowledge of herbal medicine and her constant care which helped Harriet pull through. Later, when Harriet was hit in the head with a two-pound weight, it was her mother again who cared for her. Slaves were not the beneficiaries of the recent medical techniques, and they managed by using remedies, techniques and knowledge brought from Africa. Some slaves may also have had contact with First Nations people who could have taught them about the healing properties of North American plants. Harriet taught her descendants about some of the healing plants and procedures that were successful in her experience. In one instance, a relative of Harriet's had her thumb almost severed. Harriet immediately went into the barn and got some cobwebs, which she used to wrap around the injury, and she covered it with a handkerchief. In three days, Harriet repeated this procedure. A scar was never seen at the site of the injured thumb and it worked!

Harriet is known to have prepared a poultice out of poke salad and dandelion greens and that was placed on feet to bring down swelling. For a cold, she would prepare a poultice of onions and camphorated oil which would be placed on the chest and covered with flannel. If the onion poultice was brown in the morning, that meant that the fever was broken. For warts, Harriet would use milkweed, break it open and put the milk on the problem area. The treated individual could not look at where the empty pod was thrown. This process was repeated two or three times until the wart disappeared.

Some members of her family felt that she could be credited with discovering penicillin.

> If Harriet saw a mould form on the top of the foods that the family had canned in the fall season, she would remove the mould, place it in another jar, add fresh lemon juice, honey and brandy (or bourbon), and shake it. If you got a cold, then you would get a teaspoon full of this mixture. She would say, "This is good for colds."
>
> — Marilene Wilkins, a Tubman descendant.

Harriet Tubman, by necessity, had to be resourceful. It was not uncommon for African Americans to use natural herbs and to have knowledge of their powers since they were barred from mainstream healthcare. Our common usage of Aspirin today is connected to the discovery of the effects of willow bark and leaves. The salicin that is contained in this plant reduces discomfort. Pharmaceutical drugs have a connection to herbal remedies. During enslavement, "professional" doctors would not be called for ailing black people, so through necessity, options to promote healing or to lessen painful symptoms were sought out. These experiences would be magnified during Tubman's time working as a nurse — there had never been a time when she was formally instructed on the care, assessment, and treatment of the soldiers brought before her. She was not a trained nurse, but nevertheless she was requested to carry out these healing functions and became the matron of the coloured hospital. So, despite her lack of formal training, her practical experience learned from her mother and other caregivers in her community equipped her to help heal sick and wounded people.

10

Successful Activism

Certainly the military was pleased with the efforts that Harriet Tubman had displayed. Her skillful teaching so that local women could learn a new trade in order to become self-sufficient; her nursing to keep the soldiers at their best and readiest; her recruitment of Confederate-owned enslaved Africans; her scouting so that not only key areas were destroyed, but also good use made of their stores of supplies. Then, in 1865, she was appointed to deal with some problems that arose in Washington, D.C. hospitals. At Fort Monroe, Virginia, she was appointed matron of the hospital. Her contribution was without a doubt useful and selfless. Harriet was so concerned about how others were feeling that she even gave up her stipend lest others feel she was being given special treatment. But it was not special treatment — she gave up her regular rations that she was entitled to as a soldier to avert any hostile or jealous feelings from others. This was what led her to bake pies and make ginger beer in the evenings so that these items could be sold by others while she continued to work on behalf of the government.

However, Harriet did accept the offer of good rates on the trains as supported in this letter from the Charles Wood collection:

> From General Hunter, Headq'rs Dept't of the South, Hilton Head, Port Royal, S.C. Feb. 19, 1863
>
> Pass the bearer, Harriet Tubman, to Beaufort, and back to this place, and wherever she wishes to go, and give her passage at all times on all Government transports. Harriet was sent to me from Boston, by Gov. Andrew, of Mass., and is a valuable woman. She has permission, as a warrant of the Government, to purchase such provisions from the commissary as she may need.

Harriet Tubman wanted to see her family, so with her government pass entitling her to pay half fare on the train, she retired from the hospital and headed for Auburn. Even though she had paid for a seat, her presence offended some of the other paying passengers. Her credibility was doubted — how could a black person have a government pass? The ticket taker and several men insulted Harriet, grabbed her, and threw her into the baggage compartment, badly hurting her arm. Harriet had survived the war only to receive her war injury on her way home. Her injury was to her person but also to her income, and considering that she had been a commander of about eight men in preparation for and during the battle on the Combahee, that she was fired upon and that she then performed more typical women's work on top of that, she was entitled to a reasonable bit of compensation and respect. However, unknown to Harriet, at about the same time that she was being abused, William Lloyd Garrison, a white anti-slavery worker, was receiving $30,000 for his abolition work. Clearly, despite the 13th Amendment freeing the slaves in Union territory, the treatment and experience of blacks was still not fair or equitable.

Harriet Tubman's derelict Auburn, New York, home, circa 1947.

In one example that was close to Harriet, her estranged husband, John, had an argument in 1867 with a white man named Rob Vincent in Dorchester County over some ashes. Rob threatened to kill John, and when the two happened to meet later in the day, Rob stopped his wagon, turned, and deliberately fired at and killed John before driving off. Two witnesses saw what occurred, one being John Tubman's thirteen-year-old son. Rob was tried and found not guilty.

After her arrival in Auburn, Harriet tried to raise money for two freedmen's schools in North Carolina, and asked wealthy supporters for donations, gave passionate presentations at meetings, and gave parties in order to help. To support herself, Harriet worked as a nurse, cooked, took care of children, raised chickens, grew vegetables for sale, and relied on the people of Auburn for ad hoc supplies. She would not have been in this position if she had fewer people living with her to care for. Her reputation was such that after the war, the injured, the impoverished, and the elderly, would show up at her home looking for assistance. Not willing to turn them away, she welcomed them, expanded her vegetable garden, and tried harder to seek donations from the wealthier class in town. She cared for up to twenty people, including her parents, her brother William Henry, Mary Ann's son Harkless Bowley, and a grand-niece Eva Stewart.

Had Harriet received what she was entitled to for her work with the government, which she estimated to be $18,000 (blacks routinely were paid half of what whites would expect to receive), plus an additional amount for recruiting, she would have lived much more comfortably. Later, Harriet did receive some money from the sale of the Bradford book.

Harriet was surprised to meet Nelson Davis at her door one day. He claimed to have met Harriet in 1864 while he was a member of the 8th Coloured Infantry. He greatly admired Harriet, and though he was twenty years younger than Harriet and healthy looking, Nelson was unable to work because he had contracted tuberculosis. Harriet had a commitment to help her people and may have been flattered by his admiration or felt a need to protect him because he was sick. Maybe the two just fell in love. In any event, they were wed in Central Church, Auburn, on March 18, 1869. They lived together until Nelson finally succumbed to his tuberculosis and died in 1888.

Harriet Tubman received a letter from her old friend, Frederick Douglass, dated August 28, 1868. In this letter he acknowledges the lifelong nature of her sacrifice and work:

> The difference between us is very marked. Most that I have done and suffered in the service of our cause has been in public, and I have received much encouragement at every step of the way. You, on the other hand, have labored in a private way. I have wrought in the day — you the night. I have had the applause of the crowd and the satisfaction of being approved by the multitude, while the most that you have done has been witnessed by a few trembling, scared, and foot-sore bondmen and women, whom you have led out of the house of bondage, and whose heartfelt "*God bless you*" has been your only reward. The midnight sky and the silent stars have been the witness of your devotion to freedom.

Harriet was able to purchase another property, 26 acres in 1896, adjacent to her Auburn home from the donations received from Auburn residents and from some of the proceeds of the Bradford book. It had two buildings already erected on it, was valued at $6,000, and had a mortgage of $1,700. Initially, Harriet had wanted to clear the property of debt and to open a home for girls, but as time passed, she hoped to be able to leave the property as a home for the aged. Harriet later deeded the property to the AME Zion Church of Auburn for this purpose. The Harriet Tubman Home for Aged and Indigent Colored People was incorporated in 1903 and formally opened in 1908. Harriet herself lived there for the last two years of her life. Currently, the AME Zion Church is still hoping to keep Harriet's dream of a home for the aged and a meeting place for the young alive through public support.

In 1888, Congress passed an act giving the widows of Civil War veterans a pension of $8 a month. Harriet, now a widow, resubmitted her petition with the support of Secretary of State William Seward, Colonel T. W. Higginson, and General Rufus for payment for her three years of service as a nurse, cook, and scout commander, and received $20 per month, but she was still denied a full military pension of her own. Even to this day she remains the only woman and the only black woman to have planned and carried out an armed military action against enemy forces. Mr. F.B. Sanborn, secretary of the Massachusetts Board of State Charities and supporter of John Brown said, "… she has accomplished her purposes with a coolness, foresight, patience and wisdom, which in a white man would have raised him to the highest pitch of reputation."

Her good reputation was once taken advantage of by men who wanted to profit at her expense. Harriet's brother told her about a money-making plan he had heard about and hoped that with the influential contacts that Harriet had, a profitable venture could be undertaken. Harriet's interest in doing as much as she could for the well-being of others was well known. Two black men claimed that they had been digging around a plantation and that they had found gold that had been hidden to keep it from being confiscated during the Civil War. It was a well known fact that valuables did have to be buried to keep them safe during the war. They wished to convert the gold into money and promised Harriet that she would receive a sizable portion for her aid. Harriet's credibility was high, and she was quickly able to convince her supporters of the plan's worth. She received $2,000 from Anthony Shimer and other Auburn contributors. At the appointed time, she set out with two others to exchange the money for the gold that was "understandably" too awkward to convert in the south where it had been found. Harriet was attacked, becoming separated from the others, and was forcibly bound and gagged. After all of this, neither gold nor money remained. Her dream of opening a home for black people seemed to be lost and her desperation to have adequate and surplus funds made her a victim for this unfortunate scheme.

Perhaps this incident reminded her of her own poverty and mortality, as Harriet Tubman had her last will and testament drawn up, and also met with the local authorities to again try to have her finances improved through her status as a widow. In her statement to C.G. Adams, clerk of the County Court of Cayuga County, New York, she said that she was now the widow of Nelson Davis. She indicated that they were married by Reverend Henry Fowler on March 18, 1869. She also said, "I never had any children nor child by the soldier nor by John Tubman." She went on to indicate that "He [Nelson Davis] never had any other wife but me." The affidavit, sworn by Harriet Tubman on November 10, 1894, was created at a time in Tubman's life when she had been a widow for six years and was likely growing weary of trying to pull funds together all the time.

Harriet still remained active in the community. At over seventy-eight years of age, she was supporting the growth of the African Methodist Episcopal Church, though attending the white Central Church. She attended the National Association of Colored Women's Conference and was invited to celebrate Queen Victoria's 1897 birthday party in England. Harriet received a medal and a silk shawl from the Queen, which she treasured. A benefit party was given for her by the suffragettes of Boston, and Harriet used the money raised there, plus the proceeds from the sale of the second edition of her book and money from the citizens of Auburn, to purchase the lot of land next to her house. This became the Harriet Tubman Home for Aged and Indigent Negroes in 1908.

11

The End of the Line

Harriet Tubman shortly before her death in 1913.

The once strong and active Harriet became confined to a wheel-chair because of the severity of her rheumatism and the frequency of her sleeping spells. She contracted pneumonia and died on March 10, 1913. She was buried at Fort Hill Cemetery with her medal from Queen Victoria. A marble headstone was contributed by the National Association of Colored Women, and Civil War veterans fired a volley over her grave as a tribute to her military service. One year later a posthumous honour was given to her by the city of Auburn in the form of a plaque at the Cayuga County Courthouse.

Listed on her death certificate were her living heirs and relatives, including many Stewarts in Auburn, a Robinson in Buffalo, and these Canadian relatives:

- Mary Stewart: a niece who resided in St. Catharines.

- Gertrude Thompson: a niece who resided in St. Catharines.

- Amanda Gales: a niece who resided in St. Catharines.

- Carrie Barnes: a niece who resided in Cayuga, Ontario.

- Mary Young: a niece who resided in St. Catharines.

As an additional act of respect, the citizens of Auburn unveiled a plaque on the Cayuga Courthouse dedicated to Harriet Tubman on July 12, 1914, while a tribute was delivered by Booker T. Washington. The Auburn plaque said:

IN MEMORY OF
HARRIET TUBMAN

BORN A SLAVE IN MARYLAND ABOUT 1821
DIED IN AUBURN, N.Y. MARCH 10TH, 1913

CALLED THE 'MOSES' OF HER PEOPLE DURING THE CIVIL
WAR, WITH RARE COURAGE, SHE LED OVER THREE HUNDRED
NEGROES UP FROM SLAVERY TO FREEDOM, AND RENDERED
INVALUABLE SERVICE AS NURSE AND SPY.

WITH IMPLICIT TRUST IN GOD SHE BRAVED EVERY DANGER
AND OVERCAME EVERY OBSTACLE, WITHAL SHE POSSESSED
EXTRAORDINARY FORESIGHT AND JUDGMENT
SO THAT SHE TRUTHFULLY SAID—

"ON MY UNDERGROUND RAILROAD I NEBBER RUN MY TRAIN
OFF DE TRACK AND I NEBBER LOS' A PASSENGER."

~

THIS TABLET IS ERECTED BY THE CITIZENS OF AUBURN
1914

In Bucktown, Dorchester County, Maryland, a historical sign marks the spot where Harriet received her head injury long ago — the site of the Bucktown store. In 1944, a Second World War Liberty ship was christened the SS *Harriet Tubman* by Eleanor Roosevelt as a further honour to the descendants and supporters of Harriet Tubman. In 1978, the U.S. Postal Service issued its first stamp in the Black Heritage USA Series commemorating Harriet Tubman.

The Province of Ontario erected an historical plaque dedicated to Harriet Tubman on the grounds of the St. Catharines branch of the British Methodist Episcopal Church of Canada in July 1993. This writer was honoured to have been the keynote speaker on this occasion and has participated in all Tubman commemorations since that time. This would include anniversaries, special occasions, and the most recent honour for the Canadian home of Harriet Tubman, the national historic commemoration of Salem Chapel, British Methodist Episcopal Church in St. Catharines as a national historic site by the Government of Canada in May 2011. In ceremonies leading up to the unveiling, government officials, descendants of Freedom Seekers, and relatives of Harriet Tubman joined together to celebrate her achievements and her legacy of inspiration. Work is now being done to have a Canadian Commemorative Stamp issued in honour of Harriet Tubman. The American Presidential Medal of Freedom is also being sought by her supporters.

Photograph courtesy Gregory Matthews.

The Harriet Tubman monument in Boston.

* * *

Harriet Tubman's dedication, commitment, and courage, her ability to "keep on going," no matter what the obstacles, and her genuine concern for others show her to be a woman who made a difference — to blacks, to abolitionists, and to North American history. Her example compelled others to forge their own freedom train or assert themselves in dynamic ways, because if this woman could succeed, many felt that they could too.

The following priceless narrative was provided by a Canadian descendant of Harriet Tubman. It was kept safely among her family's personal collection since it is the freedom story of their ancestors. If you map out the route, you will note that it was not direct to the shortest entry point into Ontario from West Virginia, adding to the duration and the stress involved in the escape. It is possible that routes were blocked, or that the freedom seekers needed to travel in the opposite direction to throw off suspicion that they were headed to Canada. You will note the strong motivation of the individuals to be together, to seek each other out, and to live in freedom no matter the cost.

> The Underground Railroad escape story of Lucy Canada (born: July 10, 1813) and Steven Street, as told by their daughter Henrietta Street (a Canadian Tubman connection).
>
> My mother was born in Parkers Burgh, W.V. in 1813. Her Father's name was Arion Keneday and her Mother's name was Milla Canada. Mother had Two Brothers and One Sister, her name was Melinda, Brothers were, William and George.

Their owners name was Barnes Beckwith, he being the son of an English Gentleman, by the name of Sir Jonathon Beckwith, broken down by sporting with horses, hounds and cards, and the old man kept a lot of hounds at that time. Mother often said that they were not treated like slaves, but she could not bear the thought of not belonging to herself, especially we Three Children. Our names were, as follows: Henrietta Street, Ellen Elizabeth and Andrew Clarke. Clarke was a favored young "Doctor" of the young ladies. The lady was Miss Jane Beckwith, Miss Mary and Mandy and Penelope Beckwith and Two sons, Barnes and Albert, they were all very kind, but that did not suffice. Father belonged to another man, Billy Neil. I have heard him name two or three different ones, Jonas Lewis and Frank Keene, his home (that was Father's home) was about seven miles from Mother's. His master was about to sell him when he ran away, travelling under the name of Frank Hammond, fought his way out of the hands of the oppressor and fled to the Land of Freedom, landing in Canada, at Windsor. Father left his Master's about six weeks before Mother and three children followed him, her two Brothers and a fellow servant named Nero Bansom, he being so white in complexion that he would venture out to the near by houses to seek aid while we lay in a hiding place while he found friends until we arrived at Astibula.

There we got on board a schooner and landed at Point Albino, settled in the neighbourhood of Bertie, then Mother advertised for Father and he came at once. Her Brother George came with her and saw her settled but William went to Malden. In a short time we moved near St. Catharines on a farm of one Peter Smith. There they were converted and baptized by Elder Christian of Toronto and became members of the Zion Church in St. Catharines, so in time they moved to Grand River with the intention of making a home there. And here they found the same God that had brought them from the land of bondage and in that humble cabin they erected an altar to the Almighty God to whom they served with Four others, John Taylor, Rosana Allan, Robert Bailey and Kisie Allan. Then at the age of Nineteen, Mother and Father were married, he was Twenty-six years old.

— From the personal collection of Betty Browne, a Canadian descendant of Harriet Tubman

Epilogue

As one of the most successful black women to act as a conductor on the Underground Railroad, Harriet was able to guide perhaps as many as three hundred persons in a total of nineteen trips. While there is question about the exact number of persons that she conducted and the exact number of trips made, it remains that through her courageous activity, many others were inspired to attempt to become freedom seekers or freedom leaders for others.

In later life, Harriet Tubman hinted that she may have made more than nineteen rescue missions on the Underground Railroad. It may be that her method of travel involved adjusting her route if she sensed there was a problem. For example, if she saw someone give her a second look or a questioning glance and she was travelling north, she would change her direction and head south since a person seeking freedom would not be heading into the deep south. Harriet may also have doubled back in other directions due to patrols, weather conditions, or due to an expected contact not being available. Finally, while she never lost a passenger, she may have had to remain in hiding for an extended period.

As previously discussed, pro-slavery forces constantly tried to diminish the agency that black people had, instead wishing to see them as deficient as a group. How could this illiterate woman be so able to spirit away their property? Anti-slavery forces, on the other hand, would be more inclined to overstate the effectiveness and activity of the Underground Railroad to affirm the "created equal" idea of all of mankind.

The Underground Railroad was a secret system of people helping people to be free. It remained secret, save for the staunch advocates who had risked their lives to speak out about it, or write about it. For many who were involved, their stories were not recorded or their deeds not fully shared. They were acting on their conscience and may have chosen to go about their efforts quietly and steadily — or may have helped on a single occasion without a full sense of their contribution.

The cessation of the Civil War and the passage of the Amendments did not assuage the fears that some people had about retribution or punishment, and in fact some were charged with breaking the law since providing assistance to a runaway, a fugitive slave, was against the law. Enslaved Africans seeking their freedom were stealing themselves, stealing their labour from their owners, so being a part of this theft was punishable by law. This is the reason that there are few documents to attest to the authenticity of certain places being safe houses, for example, or for objective verification of individuals' participation.

In the north, abolition took on a religious zeal, with those who were schooled in theology and well versed in the struggles of people to be free that they gave their lives in fighting slavery. It pitted north against south, blacks against some whites, the morally superior to the "others." It framed the discussion in every household, whether slave owning or not, because slavery permeated society in a broad way. Every time that Harriet was able to secret out a slave, she was breaking the law and she was making an anti-slavery statement. Even if a person was not escorted by Harriet Tubman, that person may have been informed of the linked safe houses or of a trusted contact by Tubman or by other abolitionists or free blacks. Even if the person never met Tubman, the discussions about her success would have fuelled the imagination of freedom seekers and given hope and inspiration to those about to take that bid for freedom.

Her success was the legacy of hope, not how many exact full trips she was able to travel, and not just about the exact number of persons that she conducted personally to St. Catharines. The Tubman legacy is the legacy of the Underground Railroad — a regular person could successfully find freedom in the northern United States or in Canada, an enslaved person could be freed of their bondage. It was the knowledge that it was possible; the reality that there was a place where one could be free. That is why she was named Moses: because she was able to lead her people into freedom, and also perhaps with God's presence to guide her.

The Underground Railroad was critical for the freedom seekers. It heightened the debate between slave-holding interests and those who promoted abolition. Had Canada not been willing to grant the same rights and privileges to blacks as to members of other groups, and had it not been in such close proximity to the Americans, the chance of any Underground Railroad survivors being in Canada would be scant. Freedom seekers would have had to find their way to other areas, most bounded by broad expanses of ocean and more difficult to navigate.

In the pioneer society of English speaking southern Ontario in particular, conditions supported the entry and security of freedom seekers. The first Lieutenant-Governor of Ontario was an abolitionist. John Graves Simcoe had addressed the issue of Chole Cooley, an enslaved African woman who was forcibly bound and rowed across the Niagara River onto the American side for sale. This produced the first anti-slavery legislation in Ontario to be passed in 1783. While it was a compromise, and only ended the indenture of European workers, it did provide a number of conditions for the eventual abolition of slavery within the British Empire. People in the Niagara region were aware of this precedent and it informed later treatment and acceptance of Africans. However, freedom does not always mean full equality, so it was for this reason that some people chose to return to the U.S. after the end of the Civil War. They also hoped to reunite with family that had not been able to flee.

Many black people were able to express the positive experiences of their freedom in Canada through their writing or speaking engagements. Among them were Mary Ann Shadd, Frederick Douglass, Reverend Samuel Ringgold Ward, William Still, Henry Bibb, and Josiah Henson. They were concerned about highlighting their successes because pro-slavery interests promoted the notion that black peoples could not manage on their own without paternal whites to direct their every move. It was felt that black people would be unable to lead wholesome lives and needed slavery to protect them from themselves. These black abolitionists portrayed the free black community in a positive way, showing that black people were not only competent and capable but also interested in taking care of themselves. Abolitionists travelled throughout the north and the south, speaking wherever they could find an audience, sharing information about how well the black people in Canada were managing, were thriving, were excelling. They told of the success of the black population in Ontario and these people as a group, but Harriet Tubman in particular, were a beacon of hope to the entire free and enslaved population. If they could do so well in Canada, then surely they could manage in other countries once slavery had ended.

Although there were laws protecting the right of black people under the law in Canada, there were fully entrenched views of black people that were not easily changed. In Canada, black people had to keep fighting for the full expression of their rights and where numbers warranted also opted to create or maintain their own institutions.

While Harriet Tubman is known globally for her efforts to lead people from enslavement to freedom, her role as a commander for the Union Forces is equally significant. Being the first woman to do the reconnaissance, to command a team of eight to ten men, to plan and lead a successful military action may well have given the Union side even more exposure and credibility in the minds of potential recruits, and may have given the Union side the "boots on the ground" that they needed to ensure their victory.

The onset of the Civil War prevented Harriet Tubman from using her skills and contacts for the freeing of enslaved Africans using the Underground Railroad. It did allow her to focus her energies on nursing and cooking for the sick and injured, but she also more than realized that the success of the Union Forces, no matter how President Lincoln interpreted events, would be the vehicle through which all enslaved black people could be freed.

Her role with John Brown, the fact that she supported him but in the end was unable to join him, is a turn of events that ultimately worked to enhance Harriet Tubman's legacy. Instead of being one of the persons executed following his failed bid to take Harpers Ferry, she became the person who succeeded with her own military expedition. Perhaps having his example and failure to learn from, Harriet Tubman was meticulous about working with people who she knew well and felt she could trust. She planned every possible detail in the event that something went a bit off course. She had clear goals and communicated them to the people she was in charge of. She also seemed to have been as involved in the action as anyone else. She was an organized, detail-oriented, responsible leader.

Additionally, the abolitionists, the women who supported anti-slavery initiatives, and those who fought for equality and justice, who reasoned out the nature of oppression of the enslaved black people, also determined that some of the same issues framed slightly differently applied to them. Harriet Tubman did not bring about women's rights and suffrage in the United States, but her success and example combined with their ability to add to their organizing, and contributed to freedoms for women in the United States and Canada.

Harriet Tubman's example of dedication, courage, and commitment, her ability to persevere no matter what the obstacle, her ability to develop and work her relationships, and her genuine concern for others show her to be a woman who made a difference to Africans in the Diaspora, to women, to abolitionists, to history. Her example compelled others to forge their own freedom train or to assert themselves in dynamic ways and she was an inspiration to others: if this woman could succeed, many felt that they too could succeed.

Chronology of Harriet Tubman (Circa 1820–1913)

Tubman and Her Times   *Canada and the World*

Circa 1604
Mathieu Da Costa was the first named African, a free person, to arrive in Canada. He was an interpreter for Samuel de Champlain and facilitated communication between the indigenous peoples and Europeans.

1619
The first group of enslaved Africans reached British North America, landing at Jamestown.

1628
Olivier Le Jeune, a child of about 6–8 years of age owned by David Kirke, was the first enslaved African to arrive in Canada. After being sold to a Catholic cleric, Father Paul Le Jeune, and being baptized, he was named Le Jeune, but remained a slave.

Tubman and Her Times

Canada and the World

1665
The Code Noir, a decree passed during King Louis XIV's reign, established how enslaved Africans were to be treated. It was primarily intended for the West Indies but came to be the standard globally.

1689
Slavery was given limited approval for New France by Louis XIV since colonists complained about needing more servants. Now Pawnees (indigenous people) and Africans could be kept as slaves.

1701
French fur-trader Antoine de Lamothe Cadillac built Fort Pontchartrain (Detroit) with the support of enslaved Africans.

1709
Louis XIV formally established the enslavement of Africans to meet the demands of French colonists in what is now Canada by law.

1734
Marie-Joseph Angelique, in the process of making herself free or in the process of protesting her owner's actions, caused a fire to start. This fire destroyed her

Tubman and Her Times   *Canada and the World*

owner's home as well as most of
the Montreal area nearby. For
her role in this accident, or act
of defiance, she was tortured and
hung.

1775
In Virginia, Lord Dunsmore
recognized the significant number of enslaved Africans that
could be conscripted to defend
the Crown against the growing Rebel forces. "Every person
[man] capable of bearing arms
… including servants, negroes,
or others" were to be included in
the Ethiopian Regiment. Three
hundred men joined through the
Lord Dunsmore Declaration.

1776
During the American
Revolutionary War, General
Henry Clinton extended the
Dunsmore Declaration and
invited all black persons to join
the side of the Crown in order to
defeat the rebel forces. They were
known as the Black Pioneers.
Skilled black men worked as
buglers and musicians through to
woodsmen and general labourers.

To weaken American
forces during the American
Revolutionary War (1775–
1783), the British promised

Tubman and Her Times

Canada and the World

black people freedom and land for their support upon arrival in Nova Scotia. At the time, Nova Scotia included present day New Brunswick, Prince Edward Island, and Nova Scotia. The Company of Negroes (some were free, some were enslaved) left Boston with the British and began to settle the area.

1777
Sir Henry Clinton's Philipsburg Proclamation guaranteed rebel-owned blacks who joined the British side their freedom, land, and start-up provisions. It further promised freedom to all enslaved Africans who requested protection. At least 100,000 enslaved African Americans flocked to the British side with the incentive further enhanced by British Commander-in-Chief Sir Guy Carleton promising freedom to all who formally requested it. Freedom was now possible for men and women and children for their connection to the British side.

1781
Reverend John Stuart, a Loyalist leader and the first minister established in the Church of England in Upper Canada,

Tubman and Her Times	*Canada and the World*

Canada and the World

brought enslaved black people with him that had been purchased from the Mohawk Valley.

1784
Reverend David George, a black Loyalist Baptist preacher from Virginia settled in Shelburne, Nova Scotia. There to meet the needs of the large black Birchtown settlement, his sermons were soon valued by all Christians no matter what their race. With money raised through his efforts within the black community, Reverend George established many black Baptist churches.

Tubman and Her Times

1785–1790
Benjamin Ross (owned by Anthony Thompson) and Harriet "Rit" Green (owned by Athon Pattison), the parents of Harriet Tubman, likely were born in Eastern Shore, Maryland.

1790
The Imperial Statute of 1790 permitted settlers coming into Upper Canada to bring their enslaved Africans with them as long as they were clothed and fed. Any children born to an enslaved woman was automatically deemed to be a slave and could become free

Tubman and Her Times	*Canada and the World*
	at twenty-five years of age. No enslaved person could be set free unless they could prove that they could be financially independent.

1793
The invention of the cotton gin, invented by Eli Whitney, made it faster and easier to separate the tiny seeds from the cotton fibre. Producing cotton became more profitable and therefore the interest in having more enslaved people also increased.

The first *Fugitive Slave Act* was passed and allowed for the return of enslaved Africans who managed to cross into another state.

Upper Canada's first Lieutenant-Governor, John Graves Simcoe, was shocked to learn that an enslaved woman in the Queenston area was forcibly bound and taken across the Niagara River and sold to slave traders. Fearing other slave owners would do the same thing, Simcoe sought to abolish slavery but was only successful in having compromise legislation passed limiting the length of time a person could be a slave.

Tubman and Her Times

Canada and the World

1794
Black Loyalists in Upper Canada petitioned the government to have a separate black settlement in recognition of their military service during the American Revolutionary War. While this petition was not granted, later events supported the idea of having an all black settlement based near Barrie, Ontario. The Oro settlement was created in 1819.

1796
After successfully fending off the British from taking their land for almost one hundred years, the Jamaican Maroons were finally vanquished through the use of fighting dogs. About 600 Maroons were removed to Halifax and tasked with the building of the Citadel.

1808
Ben Ross and Rit Green were married.

1808
The importation of Africans was ended by U.S. Congress

1812
Richard Pierpoint, a black Loyalist in the Niagara area, petitioned the government of Upper Canada to raise a company of black men to defend the Niagara frontier. While initially not approved, it was later decided

Tubman and Her Times	*Canada and the World*

that a company be formed under
the command of a white officer,
Captain Robert Runchey.

Americans declared war on
the British Empire on June 18,
beginning the War of 1812.

Motivated by a hatred of enslavement and the concern that the
American forces might win,
thousands of black volunteers
served to defend the British.
They wanted to have freedom
from enslavement for themselves
and their families.

1813–1816
As the War of 1812 waned, British
Vice Admiral Alexander Cochrane
extended an invitation to leave
the United States and be trans-
ported to British territories. Four
thousand black refugees accepted
the invitation and two thousand
headed for the Maritimes.

1815
The Underground Railroad
began slowly with the end of
the War of 1812 and the reputation that Canada had started to
develop regarding slaves.

1819
John Beverley Robinson declared
that residence in Canada made

Tubman and Her Times

Canada and the World

black people free and that this would be supported by the courts in Canada.

Lieutenant-Governor Peregrine Maitland of Upper Canada provided land grants to black veterans as part of a black settlement plan in the Township of Oro near Barrie, Ontario.

Circa 1820
Araminta, or "Minty," (later Harriet) Ross was born in Eastern Shore, Maryland, likely Dorchester County, to parents Rit and Benjamin Ross.

1820s
During her early childhood years, Harriet was hired out to tend to muskrat traps, babysit, and weave.

1829–1830
In response to newly introduced "Black Codes" (severe rules to restrict black activity and mobility) in Ohio, many black people from Cincinnati opted to create a huge settlement called Wilberforce near London, Ontario. Many other black settlements were smaller, and there were about forty in Upper Canada by the end of the eighteenth century.

1830
Josiah Henson, after years of faithful service to his owner, reached Canada with his family after escaping from Kentucky. Using his skills in the Dresden

Tubman and Her Times	*Canada and the World*
	area, he created a settlement to be self-sufficient for blacks by creating their own materials for sale. Fine timber was among the better products made for sale. He may have been the inspiration for the book *Uncle Tom's Cabin* by Harriet Beecher Stowe.
	1831 Nat Turner, a charismatic enslaved African, used his freedom of movement from his preaching to organize a slave revolt in Virginia. Discovered before too long, he and his followers were hung and the freedom of movement of enslaved Africans was increasingly restricted and monitored.
1834 Harriet received a major head wound in the Bucktown General Store as she blocked a doorway to prevent another slave from being captured.	**1834** On August 1, 1834, slavery was abolished throughout the British colonies, which included Canada. The act formally freed nearly 800,000 slaves but there were probably fewer than fifty slaves in British North America by that time. Enslaved people throughout the world celebrated this important Emancipation Day.
	1837 Solomon Moseby stole a horse as part of his escape from Kentucky on his way to Canada. His arrest in Newark sparked

Tubman and Her Times

Canada and the World

hundreds of supportive free
blacks to protest by standing
around the jail for three weeks
to keep him from being moved
to another facility. Finally, police
forced their way through and
in the process a riot took place
resulting in the deaths of at least
two supporters.

With the beginning of the
Mackenzie Rebellion, black
enlistees were encouraged to join
the military. When a call was
issued for volunteers by Captain
Thomas Runchey and Captain
James Sears, fifty black men
joined within four days.

1838
Lieutenant-Governor Sir Francis
Bond Head praised the brave
service and loyalty of the black
volunteers during the Mackenzie
Rebellion.

1840
Benjamin may have been freed
through the will of his owner,
Anthony Thompson, who had
died about 1836.

1841
The British North America Act
united Upper and Lower Canada
as equals; together Canada West
and Canada East, as they are now

Tubman and Her Times	*Canada and the World*
	called, formed the Province of Canada.
	1842 On a slave ship called the Amistad, Africans led an uprising as the ship was nearing Cuba. Eventually, they landed in the United States and waged a legal battle over their situation that raised awareness about the slave trade and the people being enslaved.
1844 Harriet probably married John Tubman, a free black man. This is also about that time that she became known as Harriet.	**1844** The *Globe* newspaper in Toronto and its anti-slavery/abolitionist editor George Brown used the power of the press to attack events and situations that were oppressive towards free and enslaved black people.
	1846 The Oregon Treaty set the forty-ninth parallel as the border between British North America and the U.S. from the summit of the Rocky Mountains west to the Strait of Georgia.
1847 Harriet began working for Dr. Anthony Thompson.	
1849 On September 17, Harriet Tubman escaped with her	**1849** The Elgin Settlement was challenged by the bias of Chatham's

Tubman and Her Times	*Canada and the World*
brothers Ben and Henry to Philadelphia. Edward Brodess died and Harriet learned she and her brothers were to be sold to recover some of the Brodess family debts. A runaway slave notice was published a month later in October offering a reward for their return.	Edwin Larwill. Larwill was opposed to the Elgin Settlement and attempted to organize resistance to its growth resulting in a debate with Reverend William King, a debate that turned favour towards the continuation of the settlement.

1850
The second *Fugitive Slave Act* was passed on September 18 (effective 1851).

Harriet conducted her niece to freedom in Canada.

1851	**1851**
Harriet raised money for more Underground Railroad rescues by working as a cook and a domestic in private homes and hotels in the Philadelphia, Pennsylvania, and Cape May, New Jersey, areas. Harriet returned to Bucktown to bring her husband north so they could be together in freedom, but found he had married another, so she rescued a small group instead.	The publication *Voice of the Fugitive* was published by Henry Bibb in Windsor with a focus on colonization schemes and the Refugee Home Society. The first Convention of Colored Freemen held outside of the United States met in Toronto at St. Lawrence Hall. Hundreds of black men, encouraged by the abolitionist hub that Toronto had become, joined the event, including Josiah Henson, Henry Bibb, and one woman, Mary Ann Shadd.

Tubman and Her Times	*Canada and the World*

1852
While maintaining a home base in St. Catharines, Ontario, Harriet began making several trips into slave-holding areas to conduct people north to St. Catharines. Her route took her near Albany, Syracuse, Auburn, Rochester, then over the railroad bridge and on to St. Catharines.

1853
The first issue of the *Provincial Freeman* was produced by Mary Ann Shadd, effectively making her the first black woman to found and edit a newspaper, although initially she had to conceal her identity. The first masthead indicated that Reverend Samuel Ringgold Ward was the editor, but his name was just a front for the work carried out by Shadd knowing that her gender would be problematic at that time.

1854
Using the extended break created by the celebration of Christmas, Harriet conducted three of her brothers out of Bucktown. They briefly visited with Ben and Rit in Caroline County and were assisted by the abolitionists Thomas Garrett (Wilmington, Delaware) and William Still (Pennsylvania).

Tubman and Her Times

1855
Ben purchased Rit's freedom from Eliza Brodess.

1857
Due to being accused of helping people escape, Ben and Rit were conducted to St. Catharines and lived there for at least two years before moving to Auburn, New York. Harriet was again assisted by abolitionists Thomas Garrett and William Still.

1858
Harriet met John Brown in southern Ontario and agreed to recruit supporters for his cause — a fight to end slavery.

1859
Harriet worked with U.S. Senator William Henry Seward to purchase a house on seven acres of land in Auburn, New York.

Canada and the World

1857
Through the debates connected to the Dred Scott case, it was determined that Congress could not ban slavery in the United States and that enslaved Africans were not citizens of the United States.

Navy man William Hall was awarded the Victoria Cross for his efforts to defend British interests in India. He was the first recipient and the first black man to be so honoured.

1858
James Douglas, the governor of British Columbia and himself a person of African origin, extended an invitation aimed at the black people of California to settle in Victoria. Within a short while, eight hundred black people came by boat and settled in British Columbia.

Tubman and Her Times   *Canada and the World*

On October 16, John Brown led a group of 21 men on a raid against Harpers Ferry, West Virginia. Unfortunately, the raid failed, and the men were captured.

Harriet was too ill to assist John Brown, and his famous raid took place without her active involvement.

1860
Harriet brought out seven freedom seekers, including a baby, from Maryland.

Harriet participated in a women's rights convention in Boston.

Harriet rescued Charles Nalle in Troy, New York, in broad daylight as he was about to be sent to Virginia to be charged with being a runaway slave.

1860
In the U.S., Abraham Lincoln was elected president. The Civil War broke out, pitting northern Union forces against the southern Confederates. The abolition of slavery in the South was at the heart of the conflict.

1861
The American Civil War began on April 12, with the Confederates firing on Fort Sumter in Charleston, South Carolina.

1861
The Anderson Case had aspects of slavery questioned. In the process of making himself free, John Anderson killed Seneca Diggs, who pursued him. Captured, tried, and ordered extradited, the case was handled by abolitionists who saw the case discharged on a technicality.

Tubman and Her Times	*Canada and the World*

Canada and the World

Anderson Abbott was the first Canadian-born black doctor and served on the Union side during the American Civil War.

1862
Harriet was asked to help the many "contrabands" (enslaved Africans who escaped to the Union side) in Hilton Head, South Carolina, by Governor John Andrews of Massachusetts.

Harriet acted as a scout and spy for the Union forces as ordered by General Stevens.

1863
The Emancipation Proclamation, co-authored by William Seward, was issued on January 1.

Harriet planned, and successfully carried out, a rescue mission on the Combahee River, South Carolina, which freed over seven hundred formerly enslaved Africans.

Franklin B. Sanborn wrote the first published biographical sketch of Harriet Tubman in his anti-slavery newspaper, *The Commonwealth*.

Harriet began serving as a Union nurse, cook, spy, and scout in

Tubman and Her Times

Canada and the World

South Carolina, Virginia, and Florida. She continued in this position until 1865.

1865
Harriet nursed sick and wounded soldiers at Fortress Monroe.

Harriet was injured aboard a train when thrown into the baggage compartment by a bigoted conductor who disbelieved she was given a seat. The seat was given to Harriet as part of her payment for her duties at Fortress Monroe, and she was attempting to travel to Auburn, New York.

1865
The 13th Amendment to the U.S. Constitution was declared passed on December 18 by Secretary of State William H. Seward. This proclamation outlawed slavery.

U.S. Congress created the Freedmen's Bureau to assist newly freed enslaved Africans deal with life in their new status.

Shortly after the South surrendered, ending the American Civil War, President Abraham Lincoln was assassinated in Washington.

With the end of the Civil War, the Underground Railroad essentially came to an end. While the numbers are not exactly known, at least 20,000 and as many as 100,000 enslaved Africans may have found their way to Canada, largely Ontario, on the secret routes and connections of the Underground Railroad.

1866
Mifflin Gibbs, a businessman in Victoria, helped to raise a company of black militia men and then ran for office. While initially

Tubman and Her Times	*Canada and the World*
	unsuccessful in 1862, he was later elected to the Victoria Town Council in 1866. Gibbs was the first elected black politician in Canada.
1867 John Tubman was killed by Rob Vincent in Dorchester County.	**1867** On July 1, Quebec, Ontario, Nova Scotia, and New Brunswick were officially united to form the Dominion of Canada. Sir John A. Macdonald became the country's first prime minister.
1868 Harriet submitted her claim for three years of military services and for her role leading the raid on the Combahee. Her claim was rejected at the time, but paid later.	
1869 Harriet married Nelson Davis in Auburn, New York. Sarah H. Bradford's biography, *Scenes in the Life of Harriet Tubman*, was published.	
	1870 Manitoba joined Confederation. The 15th Amendment to the U.S. Constitution was passed, giving black men the right to vote.

Tubman and Her Times

1871
Benjamin Ross, Harriet's father, died.

1873
Two men took advantage of Harriet's generosity by swindling her out of some gold and assaulting her.

1880
Rit Green, Harriet's mother, died.

1886
Sarah H. Bradford's second biography, *Harriet Tubman: The Moses of Her People*, was published.

1888
Nelson Davis died and was buried at Fort Hill Cemetery, Auburn, New York.

1896
Harriet purchased 26 acres, including several buildings, adjoining her property to create a home for the aged.

Harriet Tubman was the oldest woman to attend the National Association of Colored Women in Washington, D.C.

Canada and the World

1871
British Columbia joins Confederation.

1873
Prince Edward Island joins Confederation.

1891
Canada's first prime minister, Sir John A. Macdonald, died in office.

Tubman and Her Times

Canada and the World

1903
Harriet deeded her Auburn
property to the AME Zion
Church to continue as the
Harriet Tubman Home for Aged
and Indigent Negroes.

1905
Alberta and Saskatchewan joined
Confederation.

1909–1911
Black Oklahoma residents
accepted the invitation offered by
Canada to help to settle the prai-
ries. Hundreds were ultimately
allowed to enter since they were
of good health, had financial
resources and the skills to
develop the land although racist
attitudes tried to keep them out.

1913
Harriet Tubman died in Auburn,
New York, after her years as an
enslaved person, a conductor
on the Underground Railroad,
and a nurse, scout, cook, and
spy for the Union Forces during
the American Civil War. She was
buried at Fort Hill Cemetery,
Auburn, New York.

Selected Bibliography

Berlin, Ira. *Slaves without Masters: The Free Negro in the Antebellum South*. New York: The New Press, 1874.

Bertley, L.W. *Canada and Its People of African Descent*. Pierrefonds, Quebec: Bilongo Publishers, 1977.

Blockson, Charles. *The Black Abolitionist Papers*. Edited by C.P. Ripley. Volume 5. Afro-American Collection, Temple University Chapel Hill, North Carolina: 1985–92.

Bradford, Sarah E. Hopkins. *Scenes in the Life of Harriet Tubman*. Auburn, New York: Self published, 1869.

Bramble, Linda. *Black Fugitive Slaves in Early Canada*. St. Catharines, Ontario: Vanwell Publishing Ltd., 1988.

Clinton, Catherine. *Harriet Tubman: The Road to Freedom*. New York: Little, Brown and Company, 2004.

Conrad, Earl. *Harriet Tubman*. Washington: Associated Publishers, 1943.

Hill, Daniel G. *The Freedom-Seekers: Blacks in Early Canada*. Agincourt, Ontario: Book Society of Canada, 1981.

Larson, Kate Clifford. *Bound for the Promised Land: Harriet Tubman: Portrait of an American Hero*. New York: Ballantine Books, 2004.

Lowry, Beverly. *Harriet Tubman: Imagining a Life*. New York: Doubleday, 2007.

McGowan, James A. *Station Master on the Underground Railroad: The Life and Letters of Thomas Garrett*. Moylan, Pennsylvania: McFarland & Company, 2004.

Quarles, Benjamin. "Harriet Tubman's Unlikely Leadership," in *Black Leaders of the Nineteenth Century*. Edited by Leon Litwack and August Meier. Chicago, Illinois: University of Illinois Press, 1988, 43–57.

Sernett, Milton C. *Harriet Tubman: Myth, Memory, and History*. London: Duke University Press, 2007.

Shadd, Adrienne, Afua Cooper, and Karolyn Smardz Frost. *The Underground Railroad: Next Stop, Toronto!* Toronto: Natural Heritage Books, 2002.

St. Catharines Museum. Harriet Tubman file. St. Catharines, Ontario.

Winks, Robin W. *The Blacks in Canada: A History*. Montreal: McGill-Queen's University Press, 2000.

Index

RECYCLED
Paper made from
recycled material
FSC® C103567

Marquis Book Printing Inc.

Québec, Canada
2011

Printed on Silva Enviro 100% post-consumer EcoLogo certified paper,
processed chlorine free and manufactured using biogas energy.